ALTERNATIVE FUTURES FOR WORSHIP
The Eucharist

ALTERNATIVE FUTURES FOR WORSHIP

Volume 3
The Eucharist

Volume Editor

BERNARD J. LEE, S.M.

Authors

BERNARD J. LEE, S.M.
JOHN H. WESTERHOFF, III
JOHN C. HAUGHEY, S.J.
KENAN OSBORNE, O.F.M.
THOMAS RICHSTATTER, O.F.M.

THE LITURGICAL PRESS
Collegeville, Minnesota 56321

Cover design by Mary Jo Pauly

Copyright © 1987 by The Order of St. Benedict, Inc., Collegeville, Minnesota. All rights reserved. No part of this book may be reproduced in any form or by any means without written permission except in the case of brief quotations embodied in critical articles and reviews. For information address: The Liturgical Press, Collegeville, Minnesota 56321.

Manufactured in the United States of America.

ISBN 0-8146-1495-7

1	2	3	4	5	6	7	8

Library of Congress Cataloging-in-Publication Data

Alternative futures for worship.

Includes bibliographies.

Contents: v. 1. General Introduction / volume editor, Regis A. Duffy ; authors, Michael A. Cowan, Paul J. Philibert, Edward J. Kilmartin — v. 2. Baptism and confirmation / edited by Mark Searle ; by Andrew D. Thompson . . . [et al.] — v. 3. The eucharist / edited by Bernard J. Lee ; by Thomas Richstatter . . . [et al.] — [etc.]

1. Sacraments (Liturgy) 2. Catholic Church—Liturgy. I. Lee, Bernard J., 1932–

BX2200.A49 1987   265   86-27300

ISBN 0-8146-1491-4 (set)

CONTENTS

The Contributors   7

Preface
   Bernard J. Lee, S.M.   9

The Eucharist and Intentional Christian Communities
   Bernard J. Lee, S.M.   11

1. Celebrating and Living the Eucharist:
  A Cultural Analysis
   John H. Westerhoff, III   17

2. The Eucharist and Intentional Communities
   John C. Haughey, S.J.   49

3. Eucharistic Theology Today
   Kenan Osborne, O.F.M.   85

RITUALS

Alternative Futures for the Eucharist
Part I: Liturgy of the Eucharist
   Thomas Richstatter, O.F.M.   117

Rite 1: Weekday Assembly of an Intentional Community   132

Rite 2: Sunday Assembly of a Parish of Intentional Communities 144

Alternative Futures for the Eucharist
Part II: Liturgy of the Word
     Shared Homily: Conversation That Puts Communities
      at Risk
   Bernard J. Lee, S.M.   157

Index   175

THE CONTRIBUTORS

BERNARD J. LEE, S.M., a member of the department of graduate theology at St. Mary's University (San Antonio), has published *The Becoming of the Church, Religious Experience and Process Theology* (with Harry Cargas) and *Dangerous Memories: House Churches and Our American Story* (with Michael A. Cowan).

JOHN H. WESTERHOFF, III is an Episcopal priest and professor of practical theology at Duke University Divinity School.

JOHN C. HAUGHEY, S.J., is pastor of St. Peter's Church in Charlotte, North Carolina, with a special ministry to its business community. His most recent book is *The Holy Use of Money* (Doubleday: September 1986).

KENAN OSBORNE, O.S.F., a former president of the Catholic Theological Society of America and of the Franciscan School of Theology in Berkeley, is professor of theology in the Graduate Theological Union in Berkeley.

THOMAS RICHSTATTER, O.F.M., who has served as executive secretary for the Federation of Diocesan Liturgical Commissions, is associate professor of sacramental-liturgical theology at St. Meinrad School of Theology in Indiana.

PREFACE

Alternative Futures for Worship is not a product. It is rather a window through which a relationship may be observed. Or to change the image, it is a listening device with which a conversation may be overheard. The participants are sacramental theology, liturgical experience, and the human sciences.

All of life—like all the world—has the possibility of mediating the transformative encounter between God and human history. That is its sacramental character. In the Roman Catholic tradition there has evolved over a long history a system of seven sacraments. These are not our only sacramental experiences. But they occupy a privileged sacramental role in the life of this Christian community.

Each sacrament concerns itself with the religious meanings of some important slice of human life. There are not many slices of life whose patterns and interpreted meanings have not been probed and described by the human sciences. It is crucial, therefore, that sacramental and liturgical theology pay very careful attention indeed to the deliverances of the human sciences. Religious experience cannot, of course, be reduced to the descriptive reports of the human sciences. Yet it would be foolhardy to theologize or "liturgize" apart from serious consideration of these many empirical attempts to understand the character of lived experience in our culture and our time.

Each volume in this series exemplifies the processes of encounter between sacrament, liturgy, and the human sciences: what reports from the human sciences are being considered; how do these understandings affect the meaning structure of the sacrament; how would these meanings find liturgical expression. Every volume in the series has this fundamental agenda, but each takes it up in its own particular way. Our aims are modest; we have not intended to produce any exactly right conclusion. We only care to engage in serious, imaginative, and highly responsible conversation.

It may seem that proposing alternative sacramental rituals is irresponsible, and it would be if they were proposed for anyone's actual use. They are not! This is not an underground sacramentary. We are most aware of the tentative and groping character of each of these attempts.

However, we believe with William James that the best way to understand what something means (like this conversation between Christian experience and the human sciences) is to see what difference it makes. James says you must set an idea to work in the stream of experience to know what it means. We choose ritual as that stream of experience.

Sacramental rituals are not themselves the sacraments. The sacraments are temporally thick slices of life which through time mediate religious experience. The liturgical rite is but one moment in this thicker-than-rite sacramentalization of life. It is a privileged moment though. Ritual is a moment of high value if it illuminates and intensifies the meaning of sacrament. Leonard Bernstein's "Mass for Theatre" speaks movingly of the absurdity of ritual when it has lost touch with the lives of the people who are supposed to be celebrating it. When private meanings and public ritual meanings do not intersect (which is not to say coincide), the absurdity is thundering.

Because a ritual puts a sacramental understanding under the spotlight, we have elected to explore the conversation between sacramental life and the human sciences by imagining ritual appropriations of the fruits of the conversation. That is our way of setting an idea to work imaginatively in the stream of experience. That, and nothing more! But that is a lot.

We suggest that any readers of this volume who have not done so read the introductory volume. There we have tried to say more fully what we think we are about in this entire series and why the many authors who contributed to it are convinced that this project is a quite right thing to do. We are happy to have you listen in on our conversation. Our long-term hope is that you may join it.

Bernard J. Lee, S.M.
San Antonio, Texas

THE EUCHARIST AND INTENTIONAL CHRISTIAN COMMUNITIES

Bernard J. Lee, S.M.

One of the most important things that Christian communities have done over the centuries is celebrate Eucharist. In so doing they have understood better whence they came, who they are, and what they are called to become. The authors of this volume have wondered together out loud how Eucharistic experience might receive instruction from the deliberations of the human sciences. (What the human sciences might learn from Eucharistic communities about the nature of human community is an equally valid issue, but it does not constitute the subject of our dialogue in this volume.)

We called a weekend meeting of ourselves in early December of 1983 in Washington, D.C.: John Haughey, Thomas Richstatter, John Westerhoff, and myself. Kenan Osborne was to have joined us, but last minute concerns in Berkeley made his attendance impossible. We met without him but stayed in touch with him by phone. We already had in hand a long first draft of a manuscript from John Westerhoff addressing community, ritual life, and the American mythos. We had all read and interacted with this material, which made the meeting far more fruitful. In that meeting there was an electricity and excitement that no description can recapture. At the end of our time together we agreed upon the nature of the task at hand and how we would address it.

Then the hard work began. Each writer produced a first draft according to our agreed upon directions—a second draft for John Westerhoff, since he had already provided a significant first draft before our meeting. All of us read and critiqued each other's materials. Each made suggestions to the others about how their materials might interact more fruitfully with his own, and each made suggestions about how his material could more actively dialogue with that of the others. We continued doing that through successive drafts. It is one thing to put together four or five chapters on a related topic, and quite another to have four or five writers conspire in genuine interdisciplinary research and speculation. Let no one ever presume that interdisciplinary scholarship is easy! As editor of this volume, I have been moved by the modesty with which recommendations were tendered and the openness with which they were received. It has been a pleasure for me to collaborate with these scholars. But "scholars" does not say quite enough, for these are all people for whom the issues at hand are far from purely academic. They are people with deep commitments to the future of our churches, people whose hope for the world hangs in many respects upon Christian futures.

Two large concerns are the warp and the woof of our work: the intentional Christian community and the character of American experience as a setting for Christian life. These are, of course, not the only concerns that will be met in the pages that follow, but they are thematic, and I would like to introduce each of them briefly.

It is commonplace to observe that Christian life is communal in character. It cannot be merely private and still be Christian. However, community is one of those words in daily use with so many possible meanings that often it is nearly meaningless; that is, it has a hard time naming something quite specific. We have tried to give it a more specific meaning, an issue which John Westerhoff addresses in the first chapter. For our purposes a community always names a group of people who have two levels of concerns. First, they care about the quality of life of the individual members of the community and of their shared experience together. But, second, together they are also deeply concerned about the larger world around them and the quality of its life. They are communities of specific individuals that people freely choose to become part of. Thus they are intentional communities. Sometimes the meaning of intentional community is extended either to mean quite a large group (say, the size of a parish) or sometimes a network of smaller Christian communities. Most often, however, intentional community names smaller groupings which by their size allow individual members to develop some personal knowledge of each other.

There is a sort of implied ecclesiology underpinning this volume on Eucharist which suggests that intentional communities ideally are the building blocks of the Christian Church. It is true, of course, that a family is a unit of the domestic or local Church. Yet the family is not, sociologically speaking, a community unit. Intentional communities celebrate Eucharist together; historically this has not been a ritual expression of individual families. Our ecclesiological bias harkens to the house churches of the early centuries and also to the contemporary basic Christian communities of the South American Church, the small Christian communities of the African Church, the kinds of smaller communities in the American Church reported upon in *Tracing the Spirit*[1]—the sort of communities upon which hope for American Catholic life is expressed in two publications of the National Federation of Priests' Councils, *Developing Basic Christian Communities—a Handbook* and *Basic Christian Communities: The United States Experience.*[2]

The Rite of Christian Initiation of Adults (R.C.I.A.) embodies what Aidan Kavanagh says is a "strategic vision of the church local and universal."[3] Instruction in the usual sense continues to play a role in socialization into our Christian tradition. But the main model for the R.C.I.A. is one of apprenticeship: a candidate enters into a stable relationship with a stable community and is gradually socialized into the larger community of faith. There is an "osmosis" character to apprenticeship. Identity is gradually absorbed in the course of relational interaction in a relational web called Christian community. Kavanagh observes:

> Catechumens are to be formed by living closely with others who know well the demands and advantages of a Christian way of life. The exemplary role of sponsors, godparents, and the whole local community of faith is paramount in this mode of formation. One learns how to fast, pray, repent, celebrate, and serve the good of one's neighbor less by being lectured at on these matters than by close association with people who do these things with regular ease and flair.[4]

The lack of intentional communities to which a catechumen can be apprenticed is no small drawback to a full implementation of the strategic vision of this sacrament of initiation. We are noticing now a significant seepage out of the Church of men and women who entered through the R.C.I.A. Part of the reason seems to be that the promise of a community to which one can belong (as described sociologically above) does not materialize once the catechumen has been baptized.

It is certainly not our desire to say that the Christian Church does not exist except in small intentional communities. Yet we do not shy away from suggesting as ideal that intentional communities are the building blocks of ecclesial life. It feels more compelling to think of networks of intentional communities that grow up into a parish, rather than parishes that break themselves down into smaller community units or networked parishes that grow up into a modern diocese, rather than a diocese that breaks itself up into parishes.

Philosophically the universal exists only because of the particular instances of it. In a sense the universal Church only exists because of particular local instances of it. We are suggesting the vital importance of intentional communities as basic units or instances of Church. Indeed, as with every organism, the whole is more than the sum of its parts. The universal Church is more than a collective name for all the local Churches. It has a life and a richness that no local Church fully instances. Yet the incredibly rich reality of the universal Church accrues from the life of particular Christian communities.

John Westerhoff's chapter on "Celebrating and Living the Eucharist" offers a description from the social sciences on the nature of community to help give our common effort some functional hold on the meaning of community. John Haughey explores in detail the early Corinthian community, and with compelling insight recovers Paul's ontology of intentional community as Body. As Kenan Osborne leads us through the more recent history of how theology has explored the meanings of Eucharist, he notes those which are especially apropos to our concern for intentional community. In the alternative Eucharist rituals Thomas Richstatter imaginatively shapes his proposals to the functions of intentional communities or networks of them (though to be sure his suggestions are relevant beyond that immediate context). In a final section of the book, I have suggested how insights from hermeneutical thought can help intentional communities structure their celebration of the Liturgy of the Word.

Our second thematic concern has been to pay attention to the United States as a setting for our reflections. This too, like the focus on intentional community, is a limitation as well as direction in which to move. It is also the case that the American story is not idiosyncratic. Our experience at many points mirrors that of the larger Church. The reader is usually left to make those extensions.

John Westerhoff discusses the character of American experience in considerable detail and suggests, for better and for worse, the kind of milieu it provides as a setting for a people's religious life. This concern characterizes very much of the prolific work of John Westerhoff. Kenan Osborne notes that most major developments in contemporary Eucharistic theology have arisen out of the European Church. However, he also cites the important contribution of St. John's Benedictine Abbey in Collegeville, Minnesota, to American Catholic experience and to the larger Church as well. He notes in particular the influence of the monk Virgil Michel of St. John's upon our awareness of the deep inner connection between social justice and Eucharist in the celebrating community. Kenan also offers his own prognosis about the future of the American Eucharistic experience. Thomas Richstatter is in a singularly good position to speculate upon how the futures of Eucharistic liturgy might proceed. While he was Executive Secretary for the National Federation of Diocesan Liturgical Commissions, one of his tasks was to direct an extensive study of the response of American Catholics to Eucharist in the postconciliar Church. His introduction to the alternative rites reflects his own experience and also draws upon some of the more recent studies of the subject. The alternative rites themselves are a direct response to that experience-based sense of the American Church.

The challenge to shape a faithful Eucharistic response to the Good News of Jesus Christ is unending. We are happy to offer our work as a small part of the search for forms of community and forms of worship that are faithful to the Christ event and respectful of the cultural configuration of the daily lives we lead.

Footnotes

1. *Tracing the Spirit*, ed. James Hug (New York: Paulist Press, 1983).

2. *Developing Basic Christian Communities—A Handbook* (Chicago: National Federation of Priests' Councils, 1979); *Basic Christian Communities: The United States Experience* (Chicago: National Federation of Priests' Councils, n. d.).

3. Aidan Kavanagh, "Christian Initiation of Adults: The Rites," in *Born Not Made* (Notre Dame, Ind.: Notre Dame University Press, 1976) 119.

4. *Ibid* 122.

1. CELEBRATING AND LIVING THE EUCHARIST: A CULTURAL ANALYSIS

John H. Westerhoff, III

Introduction

One of the most significant events in the post Second Vatican Council Church has been the emergence of intentional communities as a new style of Christian congregational life. Typically prior to the council most persons participated in the Church as they would in any other cultural institution, a phenomenon which often led to unfortunate consequences in terms of faithful Christian personal and corporate life. For the Church to be sacrament in the world, alternatives to the present institutional model of the Church are needed. We have found the image of an intentional community to be particularly meaningful, and while others are faithful, none appears more useful for the exploration of our concern for celebrating and living the Eucharist.

Jesus is recorded as saying to his disciples at his Last Supper with them, "This is my body, which will be given for you; do this in remembrance of me." But do what? Do what is necessary for you to become what I have begun to make you by this action, namely members of my body to be my presence in the world. The New Testament Church envisioned itself as the Body of Christ and the fellowship of the Holy Spirit whose communion or *koinonia* signified communal life, that intentional togetherness necessary for acquiring, sustaining, enhancing, and enlivening Christian faith and life.

Through baptism persons were separated from the surrounding culture's world view and value system, confessed their allegiance to the community of the Holy Spirit, and became incorporated into the Body of Christ so as to become a sign and witness to God's reign in human history.

Through participation in the Eucharist that which happened once was "re-presented," that is, made present again. Through this action of breaking bread and sharing a cup, the community made Christ present in its midst and was itself called into Christ's presence in the world. So it is that the community was renewed as a communion, a communion with Christ and with one another. The Eucharist, therefore, was the performance of an act of an intentional community which made life in community possible. Thus communion with Christ was realized through a common intentional action of an intentional community, binding it together and empowering it to be a faith community, the Body of Christ, sacrament in the world.

In this chapter we intend first to explore some of the characteristics of our culture which both make difficult and necessitate intentional Eucharistic communities for Christian faith and life. Second, we will discuss the nature and character of an intentional community and its primary responsibility to celebrate Eucharist. Third, we will make an excursion into the nature of religious experience and the means by which an intentional community can foster our ever growing and deepening relationship with God through the celebration of Eucharist. Last, we will investigate the reasons why there is typically a gap between our celebration of the Eucharist and our living a Eucharistic life and make some suggestions on how an intentional faith community can close the gap.

Our Culture

While cultural diversity is normative in the United States, we can speak of a national core. The Church is a part of this culture, and this culture is a part of the Church. Insofar as a culture expects that its religious institutions will support and bless its understanding and ways of life, the Church has been party to this task. Some believe that the Church is so absorbed by the American ethos, that it has lost its distinctive identity and the power to transform the culture; others believe that this is not so. To be sure, however, the Church and the culture have become so integrated that the Church's identity as a community of an alternative consciousness and perception to the dominant culture is difficult to establish.

The history of the relationship between American culture and religion is extremely complex, and an analysis of contemporary American culture and Christianity is equally complex. While it may be debatable whether Americans ever lived within the context of a totally Christian ethos, few question the contention that there is no distinctive Christian ethos informing our common life in the present.

American culture has from the beginning been one founded upon the principle of pluralism; that is, it is a culture committed to the maintenance of diverse subcultures and identity conscious communities living in harmony and openness to each other. Within this complex and pluralistic American culture religious diversity has been supported and encouraged. Some religious communities have sought to identify with the culture and hence lost their distinctive identities, while others have attempted to abandon the culture and hence lost their ability to influence our common life. The goal to remain "in but not part of" the culture so as to be a constant force of cultural transformation has been difficult to realize. Today we confront a number of cultural variables which make Christian faith and life difficult. These are privatism, individualism, and secularism.

PRIVATISM

Pluralism, a central affirmation of our democratic society, defines a social order founded upon the principle of harmonious interaction for common ends among various distinct communities. As a result religious diversity has flourished, and interaction between and among the various religious traditions has both increased and been encouraged. The smorgasbord of ideologies that confronts modern Americans, each seeking an allegiance and loyalty, creates a situation which tends to lead to the conclusion that all truth is subjective and relative.

Many a person, in order to maintain a necessary set of beliefs by which to live, makes all beliefs subjective and says in effect: "all that matters is what *I* believe and do." In this situation universal principles and norms for conduct are replaced by private, contextual decision-making. Public beliefs, essential for economic, social, and political life, are often framed in terms of a lowest common denominator. All truth becomes relative, and the healthy clashing of private belief and the social world diminishes. Religious belief becomes an essentially private affair, experienced in an individualistic manner and expressed in isolation from the world.

The situation is more complex in the light of the fact that our need for national unity has tended to turn the commitment of the nation's founders to freedom *for* religious identity in an open society—the principle expressed in the doctrine of separation of church and state—into freedom *from* religious identity on behalf of civil harmony. Though we may see a change, the United States Constitution in recent years has been consistently interpreted to mean that the state is in no way to contribute to any particular affirmation of religious belief. Thus in a nation where religious neutrality is supported, the difficulty of believing tends to recede into the private consciousness, and religion becomes a highly private matter.

Surely the concept of a pluralistic society in which there is freedom for religious identity is valuable, but the isolation of individuals in matters of belief and practice is socially destructive. Indeed the reaction we see in the present to this situation, namely a new trend in which various interest groups attempt to force their beliefs and practices upon all others, is also socially destructive.

We contend that one means for addressing this issue is the formation of identity conscious intentional faith communities which can help to maintain and perpetuate Christian faith and life in a religiously plural society.

INDIVIDUALISM

Writing as early as 1897, Emile Durkheim incisively described America as the cult of individual personalities. To be a mature person in our culture is to be independent, that is, to be an autonomous and responsible agent. The value of the individual is simply assumed, making individualism both a common shared social value and the product of life in our society.

As a result we tend to be blind to the fact that each of us is part of an interactive social system and none of us can ever be self-sufficient. Because we live with the illusion that the person is an independent entity, our human drive for community, desire to live cooperatively, and need to be in relationship and share responsibility are frustrated. Thus we often seek unhealthy relationships. We minimize, circumvent, and deny the interdependence upon which human life is based. We seek private homes, separate rooms with doors, private means of transportation, and self-service stores, all of which diminish our common life. Further, the conviction that everyone should pursue his or her own destiny has resulted in emotional detachment from our social and physical environment, increased competition among the races and sexes, indifference to the poor, aggression in world politics, and the conviction that no need of the group can justify the sacrifice of the individual.

Individualism, it appears, is at the very core of the American soul. Nevertheless, the Christian faith is founded upon the concept of a communal person. More about this understanding will be found in the next section of this chapter. For now we would like to contend that an intentional community is essential for healthy and faithful Church life.

SECULARISM

A Christian understanding of the world includes two dimensions: the sacred with its proper concern for an intuitive way of knowing and for the nonmaterial, and the secular with its proper concern for an intellectual way of knowing and for the material. Over the years the sacred has been increasingly ignored and the secular emphasized. As a result our culture has become increasingly materialistic. That is, we have become an acquisitive society, a society in which possession of things is dominant and the "having" mode of existence is made normal and acceptable.

Further our culture has become dominated by a technological perspective. For the first time in human history, the earth's whole environment has been permeated by and to a large extent controlled by mechanical devices. We live in a world of technique, control, and prediction. It is a world of means rather than ends.

Our understanding of knowledge is that it is trustworthy only if it is objective, analytical, and experimental. Even human beings become objects to be investigated, taken apart, and put together again. Scientific positivism, which undergirds our technological culture, simply argues that we can claim to know only that which we can verify in a particular manner. Our culture, therefore, discredits and neglects what is eternal, surprising, and uncontrollable. As a result persons may remain religious, but in reaction to secularist religious understandings they have a tendency to become escapist, autonomous, irrational, and solely otherworldly.

An intentional spiritual community which integrates the sacred and the secular is needed to maintain and perpetuate Christian faith and life. Due to the dominance of privatism, individualism, secularism, and other factors, for more than a century some social scientists have predicted the demise of religion and its influence in our culture. Still, religious life in one form or another is an abiding human phenomenon. We humans, it appears, are by nature religious beings; we have an innate longing for cosmos or order amidst life's chaos.

Chaos appears to be an ever present human experience, but an experience most of us cannot bear. We innately respond to the threat of chaos by a thrust toward cosmos: that ideal of order where everything is arranged in proper relationship to everything else, and the whole appears to be good, beautiful, and true. We are essentially religious, because we possess a need for order, a need to make sense out of our lived experience, and a need to find answers to those questions most people eventually ask: Is there meaning to life in general and to my life in particular? What is my purpose? Does anybody care what happens to me?

The desire to moor our lives to some sort of ultimate meaning is as natural as eating. We cannot live productively without some sense of an overarching meaning for life. No matter how meaningless life may seem to be, as long as we live, our humanity tells us that life must have meaning. That is why we are haunted and driven until we can discover this meaning and live accordingly.

Religion, then, is best understood as both the quest for and the response to that which is truly ultimate. By ultimate we mean that which is fundamental to life, that which transcends the superficial world of provable fact, that which leads to some sense of a total experience in which we find a resolution for our lives, a sense of order, a mooring, and a meaning. As such religion is more than a concern for the immediate; it seeks to find or to discover an authentication for all experience—past, present, and future.

One way that people have expressed their religiousness is by describing an experience of what can be best identified as the holy— that profound sense that there is infinitely more to experience than we can explain. The word "holy" points toward that which transcends or eludes comprehension, toward an awareness beyond our ordinary perceiving and conceiving. At best we can describe this awareness as mysterious, recalling that the word "mystery" expresses a sense of ignorance deeper than that which can be dispelled by information. Indeed its proper referent is *radical* ignorance or that which we not only *do* not know, but *cannot* know through any usual means.

If we look within ourselves, we begin to see that our identity is dependent on something deeper than ourselves. It is like peeling away the layers of an onion: we eventually come to the inside. We find ourselves dependent upon that which is dependent upon nothing else; it is a feeling of absolute dependence in the presence of something which is of infinite worth or value and a sense of interdependence on each other.

It seems that the human being needs and desires communal life, and the human mind is disposed not only to rationality but also to spiritual awareness, an experience of both fascination and terror. When we acknowledge our ultimate finiteness and give over our lives to what is beyond our control, we experience a sense of the sacred. To be conscious of ourselves as communal creatures before a creative force or energy is to apprehend the religious dimension of life.

Over the last two hundred years Western civilization has struggled to comprehend the human phenomenon. Through the rise of the human sciences—psychology, sociology, economics, political science, anthropology—we have attempted to explain what being human is like. Our efforts have expanded our conscious knowledge greatly. But we still have not really plumbed the depths of the unconscious. We do not really understand what we were before we were born, and death remains for humans the final unknown. We are like a spot of brilliant light surrounded by the pitch black of our ignorance. We cannot rest content with the light; we seek to probe into the dark, to express what lies beyond our grasp. The only language available to us is that of symbol or metaphor.

Our religiousness is that which is experienced in the midst of our communal life as the holy, that which is beyond expression except in the language of symbols, that which gives us a sense of order in the apparent chaos of life. Our religion provides us with a spiritual center of security and meaning. Such faith provides roots of stability, coherence, and direction for our lives and a community which makes possible the remembrance, maintenance, and perpetuation of our roots.

However, it is important to acknowledge that this human longing for religious meaning can express itself in either negative or positive ways. Religion, while natural and necessary to human life, is not always in every expression to be valued or affirmed. Religion can support health or sickness.

Religion has sometimes been attacked quite legitimately as supportive of what people discern as the worst in human nature: intolerance, bigotry, sentimentality, self-righteousness, neurotic fantasy, rigidity, ignorance, pride, privatism, individualism, secularism. At its worst religion, which should embody "perfect freedom," can become a form of slavery.

Religion can be a healthy response to life. When religion serves our human strengths, it is best understood as engaging us in life's struggles, as being rational, as being expressive of inner control or self-direction, and as being communal.

A religion of involvement is dedicated to the pursuit of meaning and value in human life. Aware that the world cannot meet our deepest needs, religion becomes an instrument for our progressive strivings after a sense of transcendent purpose for life. Just as important, it becomes a catalyst directing our lives toward a vision of a better life. It looks to the future and uses the past as leverage to move toward that future. Tradition is alive and provides a guide toward working with God to make creation anew. And there is no discomfort in the idea that God is a surprise.

A religion of escape is easy; its demands are superficial; it gives the believer the illusion of safety. A religion of involvement is difficult and risky; its demands are profound; it points the pilgrim to a dark and dangerous road. It offers not safety but an opportunity to find new and unexpected maturity. Its adherents do not use the Church and its liturgy for escape and comfort but for challenge and empowerment. Acknowledging their own acceptance and inadequacy, their concerns are the world and the struggle for justice.

Such an understanding of religion is founded upon revelation rather than magic. Revelation is an openness to that which is hidden. It is the apprehension of experience as a whole, the affirmation of a fundamental power in society and nature for good, and the perception that life has an ultimate purpose. Religion as revelation is an invitation into fuller humanity, an attempt to bring human life into harmony with God's will rather than to manipulate the world for one's own benefit. It is the religion of a Dag Hammarskjold, a Martin Luther King, Jr., or a Dorothy Day.

The religion of involvement is an inclusive believing which takes the whole of human experience seriously. It despises nothing that God created and knows sin, not in terms of arbitrary labels but in the uncertain light of what destroys our potential humanity by distorting and denying the truth. It insists that for religion there is no division between the private and public.

The challenge faced today is to provide communal life and ritual which will support healthy Christian faith and life, that is, which keeps together the sacred and secular dimensions of human life, the communal and personal, the interior experience of worship and the exterior action of daily life, the intuitive transcendent and the intellectual immanent aspects of existence. The challenge facing our celebration of the Eucharist is to maintain this unity and provide a communal context for both conversion and nurture thereby making it possible for being in the world. But it must also have the capacity to transform the dominant culture in ways that increasingly make human life more humane.

At the very center of this process of keeping human life humane is the recognition of our natural dependence upon God and each other and the human need for community. By the birthing and nurturing of intentional communities of faith, a faithful celebrating and living of a Eucharistic life will be made possible. The subject then to which we must turn is the nature and character of such a community.

Community and the Church

Social interaction is so fundamental to human life that we rarely reflect upon its nature and character. The word community is so common in our vocabularies that we tend to assume a common definition. Nevertheless, while community is something we all experience and desire, a common understanding appears to elude us. Therefore, it will be necessary to explore the meaning of the word community, especially as it relates to our understanding of the Church. After we have investigated various issues related to the phenomenon of community, we will discuss the Church as one particular type of community and make a suggestion as to the nature and character of a faithful Church for our age, namely an intentional Eucharistic community.

In descriptions of the first century of our common era, historians denote three main types of community in the Graeco-Roman world. The first was the public life of the city or nation-state to which citizens belonged; the second was the household into which they were born or adopted; and the third was the variety of voluntary associations which united persons on grounds other than geography, race, natural, or legal ties. Among the latter were various religious groups which served as intermediate communities between primary groups—small cohesive groupings with strong ties among members, intense emotional interaction, and a wide range of shared interests—and formal organizations and institutions—large impersonal groupings based upon contractual relationships with explicit structures of rights and obligations and specific goals.

The sociologist Ferdinand Tonnies differentiated between two fundamental expressions of community, in German *Gemeinschaft* and *Gesellschaft*. *Gemeinschaft* is founded upon direct relationships between human beings; it is characterized by a high degree of cohesion, communality, and duration in time. The most obvious and historically persistent examples are kinship groups, castes, and small village communities, and guilds. The family is the archetype for this form. *Gemeinschaft* relationships involve our total personalities and focus on every aspect of our lives. Intimacy and the sharing of emotion in depth are encouraged. Behavior is regulated implicitly by custom, and there is no limit to a person's obligations to the group and its members. One gives whatever love demands, and the basis of a person's worth is founded solely on their being.

Gesellschaft, on the other hand, is characterized by indirect relationships which engage individuals in only one aspect of their being or at most only a few and take the form of tenuous, loose, and less deeply rooted allegiances and casual commitments. Such relationships do not command depth of loyalty or become fundamental to human life. There is no archetype for this second form of social life. *Gesellschaft* relationships, however, do share in common certain characteristics. Each has a particular and restricted focus; persons do not involve their total personalities. The relationships are typically neutral to emotion and do not encourage intimacy. Behavior is regulated explicitly by bylaws, and a person's obligations are specific and contractual. Individual worth is judged by performance and contributions to the group's life.

It is our contention that the Church, as an intentional community, needs to be a midcommunity existing between our primary group or the household-family in which we live and the social institutions with which we associate and in which we work. Further these intentional communities will be more like a *Gemeinschaft* community than a *Gesellschaft* community.

Having established our understanding of the nature of community, let us turn briefly to the nature of the social order. Three distinct views, individualistic, holistic, and communal, have been promulgated. According to the individualistic view society is solely a collection of individuals created to satisfy the needs and desires of the individuals who comprise it. According to the holistic view individuals can only be understood in terms of the society, that is, they have no independent status, and their personal lives are at best an extension of the requirements of the social order. And last the communal view denies both that human beings are merely a part of the social order or that the social order is merely an instrument for individual self-expression. In this view human beings are communal persons in relationship who realize themselves through their participation in social groups. In the first view voluntary associations or religious congregations are based totally on autonomous free contractual relations for individual benefit; in the second such associations or religious congregations are simply the contexts for human collectivity. But in the communal view intentional communities are necessary for self-realization and humane human life.

It should be obvious that our understanding is founded upon the latter view. However, the question remains: how does this intentional religious community comprised of communal persons relate to the culture? H. Richard Niebuhr, in his book *Christ and Culture*, describes five possible relationships between the Church and society, namely: the Christ *of* culture, Christ *against* culture, Christ *above* culture, Christ *and* culture, and Christ *transforming* culture. In terms of the two extremes, the Church of culture identifies itself with the culture and thus tends to become a mirror of the culture; its opposite, the Church against culture, attempts to remain outside the culture and thus tends to have little or no influence on the culture. The Church transforming culture is best understood as a community in-but-not-of the culture. It is an intentional community with an alternative consciousness and perception existing within the dominant consciousness and perception. As an intentional community it nurtures its alternative, critically reflects on its faithfulness, and continually reforms its life so as to maintain its distinctiveness. By so doing, this intentional community prophetically manifests an alternative consciousness and perception in the world and thereby influences the social order.

In his book *The Company of Strangers*, Parker Palmer explores the nature and character of healthy public and private life as well as their necessary relationship. He makes the case that in our day both public and private life has become estranged and sick. Most people have lost their sense of relatedness, and public life has been turned over to elected officials and governmental employees. At the same time most have lost their sense of the inward spiritual life and have turned to a private narcissistic life of escape. Palmer suggests that what is needed is a community to bridge these worlds and to create a healthy interdependence between active public life and nurturing private life. He contends that this is the Church's essential character, role, and responsibility, but quickly notes that the Church has a tendency to be a reactionary community and to assume the character—that is, the image—of the community presently denied. Insofar as we experience society as fragmented, depersonalized, competitive, and sometimes violent, persons seek a religious community which is a close-knit, warm family characterized by intimacy, comfort, affirmation, and security. The result is devastating, in that the religious community becomes a community of escape from rather than engagement in public life; it devalues and suppresses conflict rather than engaging in the resolution of conflict; it seeks homogeneity and excludes the stranger rather than seeking to welcome the stranger and create a heterogeneous community. An intentional Eucharistic community, as we envision it, encourages a healthy interaction between communal life and public life.

Another way to view the Church is from a functional perspective. Ernst Troeltsch in his book *Social Teachings of the Churches* suggests a church-sect typology for understanding the nature of religious communities. The church type he defines as conservative and established, accepting the social order although claiming dominance over it. In principle it uses the social order to accomplish its goals, thereby becoming an integral part of society. Individuals are born into such a church. The contrasting sect type is disestablished and comprised of voluntary members bound together by a common religious experience. Comparatively small as groups, such sects tend to avoid participation in the social order. Individuals unite with these sects as believing, committed adults.

Since in actual life these two types mingle and combine with each other, a number of expanded typologies have developed over the years to give a more adequate picture of the range of religious communities. Each is based on the degree of inclusiveness of the members of society and the degree of attention paid to the function of social integration as contrasted with the function of personal need. The category of denomination, therefore, emerged as that church which retains characteristics of both.

An intentional community also combines elements of both the sect and church-type religious communities, but it is not a denomination in that a denomination tends to assume the character of one institution among others. Rather an intentional community is a *mid-* or base community which integrates our life within primary groups and formal associations. These intentional identity-conscious communities share the following characteristics: a common story, in terms of a shared memory and vision, providing a consciousness and perception of life; a common authority, in terms of agreed upon norms for life and principles, to which the community points in arriving at decisions related to beliefs, attitudes, and behaviors; common rituals (repetitive symbolic actions), in terms of rites of initiation, intensification, and transition, which provide us with a means for being at home in the world and a stimulus for purposefully living; and a common life together, in terms of nurturing and caring, which can mediate between our public and private lives.

The Church, we contend, can be such an intentional community, a human association of a particular kind which exists between and bridges life in our family/household and life in the society. Such an intentional community is not a "natural" association such as a kinship group; it is not a volunteer association based on self-interest such as the National Education Association, the United Auto Workers, or the American Medical Association; it is not a public service institution such as a corporation. The parish church as an intentional Eucharistic community is called to be something and do something on behalf of everyone, that is, to be a community engaged in making and keeping life humane—which means, of course, being a community of cultural transformation.

There are two kinds of movements which contribute to social change. The first are messianic movements which anticipate a change of social conditions within history, some of which focus on the reestablishment of a past ideal and some which focus on a future ideal. In these movements dissatisfaction with the present encourages the community to act in ways that will hasten the coming of an ideal past or future. All such messianic movements are action-oriented and demand intense commitment and unconditional faith. There are also eschatological movements which anticipate a better future beyond history. The interesting fact about Christianity is that it combines messianic and eschatological commitments. However, typically one or the other elements has been dominant so that our eschatological focus has tended to be escapist, and our messianic focus has tended to be sectarian. The Christian ideal unites past and future; it is both in history and beyond history. An intentional Eucharistic community supports this view.

The most helpful clue for clarifying how these two modes can be integrated is discussed by Bruce Reed, a sociologist at the Grubb Institute in England. In his book *The Dynamics of Religion*, he images life as a process of oscillation in which persons move back and forth from the structured, rational world of work to the antistructured, intuitive world of worship. The Church encourages this movement between what he calls intra- and extradependence to occur in regular and controlled ways for the benefit of society. Ritual, he explains, plays a particular function in this natural and necessary movement between two forms of dependence. Ritual properly focuses our dependent needs for meaning on God (extradependence) and thereby provides inner strength (intradependence) for purposeful life in society.

However, if the Church's ritual life denies these extradependent needs or keeps persons dependent upon the community, it no longer serves a healthy purpose. Human life as lived is not so much a series of linear events leading toward a goal as it is two alternating modes of experience, each having its own validity. Our ability to deal with the demands of life is related to our having someone on whom to depend as we move from mastery over our environment to resourceless dependence, from ego control to letting go.

Religious communities can be functional or dysfunctional. They are functional when they facilitate society's adaptive processes and hence encourage the welfare and development of the social order, aiding its people to make transitions from extradependence and intradependence. Functional religion enables persons to acknowledge, accept, and confront the chaos of life. It further engages the imagination, brings persons into contact with the one who transforms chaos into meaning, despair into hope, torment into peace, sorrow into joy, death to life, brokenness into wholeness, and sends forth new persons with new vision and power.

Dysfunctional communities encourage regressions into withdrawal or denial, fail to comfort affliction, and provide a fantasy world of escape. They also encourage activity in churches to be only a sign of devotion and provide no transition to intradependence. Functional religion is known by its fruits. If religion has no prophetic imagination, it becomes dysfunctional.

Worship can become so human that it denies the transcendent, or it can emphasize awe and mystery to a degree that it denies immanence. Apostolic religion enables persons to face their human predicament, brings them into touch with the realities of the external world, and prepares them to become involved in the affairs of the world. The supportive functions of community life and multitudes of activities can prevent the oscillation process and turn people in on themselves. The human pilgrimage is one of movement back and forth between structure and antistructure, between global structure and communion, between extradependence and intradependence. So it is that the celebration of the Eucharist is the primary responsibility of our intentional community of Christian faith.

The test of our rituals' vitality is found in their ability to take both modes of life seriously and to aid persons to move from having their extradependent needs met, to transforming chaos into order, and returning them to the world to live in an intradependent mode.

A religious view looks for the meaning of everyday reality by looking beyond what is given to a more all-encompassing reality. Through ritual a total person is engulfed and transported into another mode of existence. In ritual the world as lived and the world as imagined fuse, thereby providing a transformation in one's sense of reality. Thus it is out of the context of concrete acts of religious observance that religious convictions emerge.

Ritual is the means for providing the conviction that religious concepts are true; it also makes the culture's ethos reasonable and makes sense of unwelcome contradictions in life. Rituals are symbolic actions expressive of the community's symbolic narratives or sacred stories. These expressions move toward interpreting and understanding the meaning and nature of life, and within our rituals the common life of the community is acted out in the context of remembering, "re-presenting," and anticipating its memory and vision. Our rites are at the center of human life, binding past, present, and future together. Without meaningful and purposeful rituals daily life cannot be made or kept fully human.

The Church, as an intentional Eucharistic community, needs to reform its rituals or liturgies by providing a context for people to acquire, sustain, and deepen Christian faith, understood as a particular perception of life and their lives; by providing meaningful common rituals that make known a common memory, vision, and authority; and by providing shared intimate life.

Thus far we have concluded that the congregation which will be most faithful in our day needs to be a particular sort of intentional community which aids persons to oscillate between intradependence and extradependence. Such a community realizes that the celebration of the Eucharist is its primary responsibility and that its program and organization are secondary. But celebration of the Eucharist in an intentional community needs to be an expression of our best understanding of religious experience.

Religious Experience, Community, and Worship

Having explored privatism and individualism in terms of intentional community, we now turn to some issues related to secularism which are important for Eucharistic community and intentional communal life.

Two and a half centuries ago a struggle emerged within the faculty of Saint Thomas' School in Leipzig, an unresolved struggle which still marks a schism in the soul of the Church. It was a conflict between the school's cantor, Johann Sebastian Bach, and its rector, Johann August Ernesti. Ernesti, a pioneer in the literary, historical, and critical study of the Scriptures, believed the students should study more and sing less; Bach thought faith and its musical expressions more important. Here we see a tragic conflict between the last and most mighty musical representative of the age of faith and the younger protagonist of the age of reason and science. Two epics, two cultures, two understandings were at stake. Ernesti wished to make the study of religion the sole purpose of the school. Bach tried to defend the position that the biblical text was designed to release within the reader an intense sort of spiritual activity: faith. Ernesti chose a rationalistic, analytical, intellectual perspective on knowing, while Bach chose an intuitional, experiential perspective. Since those days the rationalists, with their emphasis on theological reflection and their interest in the literary, historical, critical method of biblical study, have dominated the Church's life. This regretful overemphasis on the intellectual mode of consciousness has contributed to the demise of the intuitional mode and contributed to a sickness in the life of the Church.

A healthy understanding of religion and human life necessitates an acknowledgment of the bicameral mind and a comprehension of its functioning. There are two interdependent ways of knowing, two interdependent modes of thinking, two interdependent dimensions of consciousness. One is an intellectual way of knowing, a rational way of thinking, an active mode of consciousness. As such it offers an objective-reflective means to knowledge. Explicit in its concern for product content and dominantly verbal in its mode of expression, it is at home in the world of order, structure, and certainty. While linear and argumentative in style, it is best suited for engaging persons in logical analysis, prediction, and control. The alternative is an intuitive way of knowing, an affective way of thinking, a passive mode of consciousness. As such it offers a subjective-experiential means to knowledge. Implicit in its concern for process content and fundamentally nonverbal in its mode of expression, it is at home in the world of chaos, antistructure, and ambiguity. While wholistic and sensuous in style, it is best suited for supporting the imagination, mystery, and discovery. It is the artificial separation of these two modes of consciousness; the depreciation among some of the signative, conceptual, and analytical aspects of life; and the benign neglect among others of the symbolic, mythical, imaginative, and emotive aspects of life which have contributed to our present religious situation in the Western Church. A religious person has developed fully both modes of consciousness and has learned to integrate their functions. Christian life has a symbolic-signative, mythic-conceptual, imaginative-analytical, and emotive-informational character.

While healthy religion has an essential rational component, we need to be aware that the essential core of Christianity—the experience of God—is in danger of being lost under a cloud of rationalizing. At the heart of Christian faith is a nonrational element that cannot be conceptualized or turned into discursive speech, though it can and must be communicated. To paraphrase Amos Wilder in his book *Theopoetic*, imagination is a necessary component of all profound knowing and celebration; all remembering, realizing, and anticipating; all faith, hope, and love. When imagination fails, doctrines become ossified, witness and proclamation wooden, doxologies and litanies empty, consolation hollow, and ethics legalistic.

An overemphasis on the intellectual mode of consciousness has contributed to the demise of the intuitional mode and contributed to a sickness in the life of the Church. It is the significance of the world of symbol, myth, and ritual that must be recaptured in our day. Religious symbols are comprised of action symbols (sacraments), narrative symbols (myths or sacred stories), and language symbols (words). Still at the heart of the matter is the experience itself, and without the experience from which the symbol emerges and to which the symbol points, words remain conceptual verbalizations requiring definition and have no power over our present lives.

In 1963 Sir Alister Hardy, the renowned British scientist, in his Gifford Lectures challenged his fellow scientists to take seriously the fact of religious experience as a central feature of human life. Rising to his own challenge, in 1969 he founded the Religious Experience Research Unit at Manchester College, Oxford. A decade later he published *The Spiritual Nature of Man*, the most seminal analysis of the phenomena of religious experience since that of another Gifford Lecturer, William James. Hardy's successor, Edward Robinson, in his book *The Original Vision*, reports on their findings concerning the religious experience of childhood. Few existing books offer greater insights for understanding religious life and spiritual awareness. To summarize their findings, a significant number of persons report having religious experiences as young children through nature, the arts, and ritual, but testify that they were unable to name, describe, explain, or understand them until much later. Because children could not talk about their experiences, it was assumed they did not have them.

Religious thought is grounded in religious experiences. Our conceptualizations of God are grounded in our knowledge of God. Our personal encounter with that ultimate mystery which is God is expressed, communicated in, and nurtured through dance, music, drama, poetry, painting, sculpture, and film; and through the stimulation of the imagination by our visual, oral, and kinetic senses. Religious experience and the arts are related, so are religious experience and liturgy. Through ritual, our subjective-experiential-intuitive mode of consciousness, the religious imagination and the religious affections are enhanced and enlivened. The distance we have put between ourselves and the arts in the Church has impoverished our religious experience and diminished the effectiveness of both our liturgies and our catechetical ministries. Our personal encounter with that ultimate mystery which is God is nurtured, expressed, and communicated through dance, painting, music, sculpture, poetry, and drama, especially as they are expressed in liturgy.

Religious life and artistic life go hand in hand. Religion belongs to the sphere of the unsayable, the absurd, the world of nonsense, which if it is to be put into words at all, must use metaphorical images, symbol words, poetry. Until we can restore the religious affections to their proper role in human life, we will remain captive to our conditioning and separated from meaningful relationships with God, self, neighbor, and nature.

We also need to take more seriously the importance of social narrative. Richard Adams' novel *Watership Down* is an adventure story about rabbits, which is really about the conditions necessary for a viable community. *Watership Down* begins with an exodus, a hazardous journey in search of a new home, ultimately *Watership Down*. The rabbits leave as a group of separate individuals, each with their own reasons for leaving. They become a people—a community—as they acquire a story, and they remain a community so long as they retell their story. Our identity is dependent on having a story that tells us who we are; our understanding of life's meaning and purpose is dependent on having a story that tells us what the world is like and where we are going.

Stories are concrete and particular; they are not open-ended, but they are not to be read literally. As a matter of fact, stories give the storyteller freedom in their retelling. Stories stimulate the imagination; there is not only one interpretation of a story. Indeed the listener is encouraged to listen freely and discover personal meaning. Stories are experiential; they are told by a participant, and they are to be participated in. Stories are the bottom line of human communal life; that is, nothing less is ultimately needed. For a story to hold our attention, it must entertain and arouse our curiosity, but to enrich our lives it must stimulate our imaginations and provide us with ever new and deeper meaning. Stories emerge from and speak to our responsive, intuitive consciousness. Sacred stories speak to our deepest, unconscious longings and questions, our problems and predicaments, our inner and outer struggles in human life. They exist in the form of truth that only intuition and imagination can provide, truth just as significant and real as that which comes through logical analysis and scientific probing.

It is human nature to order our lives in accordance with a story. Stories make sense out of the chaos of life on the level of the unconscious. Stories are of central importance in human life, and they are enacted through our rituals. We humans cannot live without ritual; our religious life is expressed collectively through symbolic narratives (sacred stories) more important than our ceremonial life. We humans are made for ritual, and our rituals make us. No community exists without a shared story and shared repetitive symbolic actions. Our understandings and ways are invariably objectified in ceremonial observance. Faith and ritual, then, cannot be separated. That explains why, when the prophets sensed that the people had forsaken their faith, they attacked the rituals as empty substitutes. But when the people had lost their faith, the prophets called them to return to their rituals. Without rituals we lack a means for building and establishing purposeful identity; we are devoid of any significant way to sustain and transmit our understandings and ways. Rituals, like stories, emerge from and speak to our intuitive, emotional consciousness.

Part of the problem, however, resides in our Western culture, especially post-Reformation Enlightenment culture which is ocular in nature. Ours is a book-oriented culture that reads and writes, thereby understanding perception primarily as seeing. As a result it turns sacred story into historical event and doctrinal conviction. It produces literalists and fundamentalists, folk who often use the biblical story pornographically (by turning a subject into an object) and as idolatry (a means turned into an end).

Our capacity for culture and our capacity to use symbols are closely connected. Our symbols affect the way we perceive and respond to our environment. As symbols are an interpretative filter, they both express and shape our experience. Symbolic relevance means the ability of the ritual to engage its participants at a level of their consciousness which awakens their sensibilities. Liturgy pertains primarily to a receptive, intuitive way of thinking. It forms and alters the social drama which people live out unaware of its motivation. Ritual, therefore, can become a retreat from reality, an attempt to compensate for moral misdeeds by cultic deeds, or a means to avoid the cost of discipleship by becoming a disciple of the cult. Prophetic criticism is not an attack on the cult but upon worship that finds no expression in social righteousness.

Ritual shapes our identity and provides us with a positive sense of self. It establishes our world, provides meaning for past stories to explain the purpose of life, provides a vision of the future, undergirds an imagination of the world as it is to be, provides metaphors by which we can talk about and make sense of our world in the present, creates community, and provides motivation for life.

While anthropologists define ritual in various ways, for the purposes of this chapter ritual is defined as repetitive, symbolic actions expressive of a community's myth or sacred story. Anthropologists further divide rituals into two classes: intensification or communal and transition or passage rites. This chapter deals solely with a single rite of intensification, the Eucharist, which like all such rites follows the calendar, binding a people into community, establishing meaning and purpose for their lives, and both sustains and transmits to the next generation that people's world view and value system.

A community's daily life is comprised of signs, concepts, and reflective actions. Manifested and participated in through predominantly cognitive modes—logical rational analysis (or its developing states), reflection on experience using discursive language, and moral decision-making and action—a people's daily life encourages ways of thinking and knowing. As such it assists them in arriving at doctrinal convictions, influences the meaning they make of their experiences, and helps them develop a conscience, that is, their intentional efforts to make reasoned judgments on what is true and false, and what is right and wrong.

All anthropologists agree that healthy personal and social life necessitates a positive link between cultic and daily life, between ritual and belief, and between a people's worship and their personal and social relationships. However, there is no agreement as to how these two do in fact relate to each other.

Two schools of anthropological interpretation exist. One views ritual as symbolic actions which shape our beliefs and the other views ritual as symbolic actions which express our beliefs. The "ritual-as-action" theorists maintain that since beliefs are rational explanations of experience resulting from participation in rituals, we must begin with ritual practice, that is, the actual ceremonial behaviors of a people if we are to understand their beliefs. The "ritual-as-belief" theorists hold that religion is an outgrowth of speculative thought and therefore maintain that our understanding of people's rituals is derivative from a knowledge of their conceptual belief and value system. We, therefore, need to comprehend a society's theological formulation if we are to make any sense of their rituals. Anthropologists such as Jon Christopher Crocker have attempted to demonstrate how the two anthropological theories are mutually complementary rather than antithetical to each other.

Sacramental theologians maintain two similar interpretations. The Latin *lex orandi lex credendi* may be construed to mean either the rule of prayer is the norm of belief or the rule of belief is the norm of prayer. That is, either worship governs life or life governs worship; worship determines doctrine or doctrine determines worship.

To resolve this interplay between cultic and daily life, sacramental theologians suggest a hermeneutical circle in which worship is the source of doctrine insofar as it is the context in which God makes

Self known to humanity in a saving encounter, and doctrine is the source of worship insofar as the rational reflection or critical examination of the fruits of worship provide us with a necessary means for the shaping and reshaping of our worship.

From a social historical perspective we move from daily life to cultic life, and from the experience of persons living in community, from cultic life to daily life. Societal change and ritual change go together. Change in one produces change in the other. Ritual, however, faces the problem of making change meaningful both by being relevant to contemporary life and providing roots in a timeless past.

To summarize, we have investigated the significance of both the intuitive and intellectual ways of knowing and have emphasized the importance of both, but have singled out the special importance of the intuitive for religious experience. We have discussed the relationship of sacred narrative or story to religious experience, community, and ritual as well as the character of good ritual. We have further explored the nature and significance of ritual in the life of an intentional community. We now turn to the reasons for the gaps between our celebration of the Eucharist and our daily lives to discover how an intentional faith community can close the gap by reforming its Eucharistic celebrations.

Gaps Between Ritual and Life

Cultic life and daily life are intended to be integrated. Often they are not. The reasons are complex and multiple. We will explore those most closely related to our culture's characteristics of privatism, individualism, secularism, and most essential for a healthy intentional Eucharistic community.

Psychosocial Pathologies

The fact that persons participate in a community's cultic life does not mean that they do so in healthy ways.

Religion is both natural and necessary for human life, but the human longing for religious meaning can express itself in both negative or positive ways. It is important, therefore, to distinguish between two functional types of religion, one that is inclined to support health and one that is inclined to support sickness. The first type might be called "the religion of involvement" and the second type, "the religion of escape." These two types are described in detail in *Christian Believing* by Urban T. Holmes and John H. Westerhoff.

For the sake of this analysis it is only important that we describe the latter.

Religion can serve human weakness. When it does, it is best understood as an escape from life, an irrational emotional longing, and an expression of an unconscious desire for a parental authoritarianism. Persons can use the cultic life of a community to support these pathological needs; participation in ritual can be escapist. No matter what the intention of the ritual, some people will use it to provide support for or protection from the dimensions of their lives in which they feel inadequate.

Further, a "religion of escape" can be seen in the difference between religion and magic. Magic implies ritual actions performed either to get something from God that we would not if we did not perform the act or to convince God to do something that God would not do otherwise. Religion, on the other hand, involves opening ourselves to God's will and celebrating an awareness of what God has already given us or done for us.

While a healthy use of ritual supports is expressive of mystery, a sick use of ritual encourages and sanctions an escape from the enigmas of life, irrational beliefs, and avoidance of moral witness amidst injustice.

The fear of the secularization of the Church may result in an unhealthy sacralization. When this occurs, we often find a clericalism which divides the work and witness of the laity from ritual participation.

To summarize, an estrangement between cultic and daily life may exist when people either produce a pathological split between the sacred and the secular or maintain a pathological approach to the use of ritual for escape.

CONFLICTING RITUALS, WORLD VIEWS, AND VALUE SYSTEMS

Each day we are confronted by conflicting world views and value systems, each striving to gain our loyalty. The fact that we participate in the Church's cultic life is no guarantee that it will be the fundamental influence in our life. For some the Church's cultic life will be so central to their being that their participation in other rituals will have minimal effect. For others the Church's cultic life will be peripheral to their being, and other rituals will significantly influence their world view and value system.

In the course of one's life, a person in our culture will participate in a large number of diverse rituals, many of which express radically divergent world views and value systems. There are political rituals such as peace marches and Republican party dinners; there are economic rituals such as labor strikes and office parties; there are civic rituals such as Mardi Gras and the Fourth of July; there are school rituals such as commencement and the Friday beer blast; there are entertainment rituals such as movies and the disco; there are television rituals such as the "soaps" and advertisements; and there are athletic rituals—perhaps the most powerful and significant—such as football. In most cultures athletic events are important cultic acts, which may help to explain why a catechumen in the early Church was required to avoid the "public games."

Each of us constructs a value system, that is, a hierarchy of values to aid us when any two values are in conflict. For example, many persons value both freedom and equality. However, most of our cultural rituals assert that freedom is the higher value. They also support individualism and individual rights over community and social responsibility, competition over cooperation, aggression over nonaggression and ownership and possession over stewardship.

The power and effectiveness of cultural rituals to support and transmit a world view and value system make it difficult for the Church's cultic life to be a dominant influence in the daily lives of its participants. The issue is made more complex when we realize how often the Church has fallen prey to celebrating overtly cultural values.

To summarize, the diversity of rituals in which people participate makes it difficult to evaluate the influence of the Church's cultic life. The world view and value system sustained by the culture inform a person's cultic life in the Church and thereby diminish the power of its influence. The variety of legitimated rituals present in the culture produces a relativism which further diminishes the effectiveness of any one ritual in the lives of its participants. Only a committed intentional Eucharistic community will adequately address this situation.

CULTURAL PLURALISM AND CULTIC INADEQUACIES

Culture is so much a part of our lives that we are unaware of it until we find ourselves in another culture. A visit to Latin America, Africa, or Asia produces the experience of culture shock. We forget, however, that there are numerous distinctive cultural differences to be found in the United States. Some are regional: there is a significant difference between Southern culture and that of the

West Coast. Some are nationalistic: there is a difference between Mexican Americans in Texas and Vietnamese Americans in New York. Some are racial: there is a difference between black and white culture. Some are socioeconomic: there is a difference between rich and poor, and so on. What are obvious, accepted, and expected understandings and ways of behaving in one group are strange and confusing in another. While from one perspective all of us in the United States share a common culture, from another perspective we exemplify tremendous cultural differences.

In any case how we understand the relationship of the Church's cultic life to culture will be dependent on which of these views we maintain. For us neither the avoidance or absorption into culture is satisfactory. The Church must incarnate itself in culture. The mystery of this incarnation, however, also questions an uneasy synthesis or inherent conflict. The relationship between the Christian cult and a native culture involves a continual interaction in which it is understood that both are under judgment and in need of continual adjustment. A people's cultic experience must be with their cultural comprehension, but it must also infuse into their culture the impetus for continual reform.

One of the reasons why cultic life and daily life may be estranged is that we have created a cultic life that is inadequate, that is, it is either too unrelated to the culture or too much in harmony with it.

The Eucharist must be celebrated within some cultural expression. The question is: to what extent should we respect a people's culture and adapt the ritual to their cultural way? The history of the Church is the history of both cultural adaption and cultural imperialism. Both are inadequate and result finally in a split between our celebrating and living the Eucharist.

The Second Vatican Council's program of liturgical renewal as outlined in the *Constitution on the Liturgy* assumes that while the new Eucharistic rite is a model for the entire world, it is to be adapted to the particular genius of every culture. Unity but not uniformity is to be the norm. Correspondence between a people's culture and the Church's ritual is assumed. If cultic life and daily life are to be integrated, a people's culture must be taken seriously. However, since adaption is to be understood in terms of Christ transforming culture, its realization is full of difficulties, any one of which when acted upon can manifest itself in cultic inadequacies and a resultant split of cultic from daily life.

Anscar Chupungco, O.S.B., in *Cultural Adaption of the Lit-*

urgy outlines two forms of adaption: acculturation and enculturation. Acculturation is the process by which cultural elements which
are compatible with the Eucharistic rite are incorporated into it.
For example, prayer in one culture may be sober and direct, in another, dramatic and elaborate. Translations of texts can be used
in terms of dynamic equivalents rather than literal parallels. The
same principle can be used in terms of symbols and symbolic actions.

While acculturation modifies the ritual by using established cultural elements, enculturation attempts to change the culture by in-
fusing its cultic ways with Christian symbols and myths. Its aim
is to imbue the culture with the spirit of the Gospel. Together acculturation and enculturation maintain the principle of correspondence as we have described it, but neither is simple.

The problem is complicated when attempts at enculturation are
made. Ritual reform has been attempted while maintaining the old
altar against the wall, the altar rails, the pews, the stained glass
windows, the statues, and the votive candles. Insofar as many
people's identity is tied up with the old space, their world of memories, associations, and feelings remains intact.

Further, while the Church intended to move toward a communal
style of life, it used institutional means to achieve it. Reform was
instituted from above as had been accepted cultural practice. The
involvement of the laity in the life of the Church was desired, but
so were accepted cultural ways. The root metaphors which under-
lie the new rituals were radically different from the old root
metaphors, but people still involve themselves in the old script,
resulting in disorientation.

To summarize, if cultic life and daily life are to have correspondence, we must discover a way to keep the universal character of
the Christian faith while making it relevant to the particularities
of culture. Some adaption of cultic life to the culture is necessary
in an intentional Eucharistic community, but that adaptation must
make possible the transformation of culture. When these attempts
are inadequate, they result in a split between our celebrating and
living the Eucharist.

Cultic Insincerity

Cultic life is essentially an intuitive, imaginative activity in the
arena of aesthetic sensibility. Knowing, in the first instance, is tacit
and personal, encompassing "mystical" experience. There are states
of insight into the depths of reality which cannot be plumbed by

discursive logic. There are illuminations and revelations full of significance, which while essentially nonrational are not irrational, romantic, or unreal.

Enlightenment Christianity, with its concern for the intellect and morality, has sometimes been insensitive to experience and the affections. It has on occasion ignored the fact that we cannot make sense of that which we have not experienced.

Margaret Mead suggests that Christian rituals are designed to evoke a feeling which is representative of the affections identified with the primal event of Christ's life, death, and resurrection. Every ritual is properly an anamnesis. Ritual is a bundle of symbols, symbolic acts and a symbolic narrative whose aims are to transport the participant into the reality to which they point. The experience of the reenactment of the community's primal event is intended to affect the participant, that is to draw participants more closely into union with Christ and thereby affect their daily lives.

We must be careful that our cultic life is not dominated by the discursive, the rationalistic, and the prosaic. Good ritual focuses primarily on the role of the symbolic and the prerational. This is not to defend a shallow aestheticism or emotionalism, but to suggest that our rituals are often characterized by too much discussion, talk, stereotyped actions, mundane music, unimaginative drama, nonexistent dance, and naturalistic art.

Good ritual should awaken the artistic consciousness. The story we "re-present" through music, dance, dramas, poetry, painting, and sculpture should touch our human story in its depths and illumine its meaning.

To paraphrase Thomas Merton in his book *Conjectures of a Guilty Bystander:* today with a myriad of instruments we can explore things we never imagined. But we can no longer see directly what is right in front of us. The core of our spiritual problem lies in our Western tendency to externalize and objectify.

It is in the imagination that culture and history are broken. We should remember that human nature and human societies are more deeply motivated by images and visions than by ideas, and by experiences more than by dogmas.

CULTIC INEFFECTIVENESS

When the Hebrew prophets denounced the people's worship, it was because it belied their conduct. Perhaps that helps to explain why in the history of the Church, whenever the community discerned that its people were not living the Eucharist, it sought to reform its celebration of the Eucharist. Indeed the history of the Church can be best understood from the perspective of liturgical reform.

Today, as in the fourth, eleventh, and sixteenth centuries, the Church is engaged in a significant movement to reshape its cultic life in order to effect more faithful daily life.

Insofar as the celebration of the Eucharist fails to produce appropriate fruits in the lives of participants, the ritual must be examined to see whether or not it is being faithful to its intentions. This has been done in our own day, and as a result a number of significant reforms have been made. To demonstrate the ineffectiveness of the older cultic life and the hope of more effective cultic life, I will discuss briefly some of the reforms.

The nature of myth as sacred story and the integration of *the* story with *our* story was for all intents and purposes lost. With the reform in the lectionary and a new attention to living the eternal cycle through the ritual as an expression of the human spiritual pilgrimage, a new synthesis of cultic and daily life is intended.

For too long we Christians came to church as observers at a ritual controlled by the clergy. The new rituals demand participation and hopefully will help people to understand that life as celebrated and lived should be consistent.

Further the social dimensions of human life were ignored through the encouragement of private, pietistic actions. As might be expected, social action on behalf of peace and justice did not follow naturally. The ritual provided a place to pray one's own prayers, and similarly daily life became the context for isolated life. The communal nature of the new Eucharistic ritual intends to change that behavior.

The reforms needed are those which make the ritual effective, which means closing the gap between cultic and daily life. While such reforms cannot guarantee more faithful life, they need to intend that effect. What we do when we gather for worship must be consistent with the life we intend to have lived day by day.

To summarize, it is necessary continually to reform our cultic life so that it corresponds with our understanding of Christian daily life, or else we will witness a disjuncture that is undesirable. The effectiveness of our cultic life is judged by the fruits it bears in our daily life. The process of keeping the two in harmony is never ending.

CULTIC ESTRANGEMENT

Last, there needs to be a reflective dimension to our communal celebrations. While intuitive relational experiences are foundational to the celebration of the Eucharist, intellectual critical reflective activities are necessary if we are to connect ritual and daily life.

An intentional Eucharistic community needs to provide opportunity for persons to reflect on their daily lives and prepare for meaningful ritual. Thus attending persons need an opportunity to reflect on God's word to them in the Scriptures and God's action at the Eucharist so as to prepare for purposeful, faithful life in the world.

Not only must our celebration be related to our daily lives, we need to be critically reflective about our lives in the light of the Gospel. An intentional Eucharistic community can do this best, and our reform of our rituals needs to encompass this need.

Summary

The Church needs to become faith communities that exist between the family and the society and its related institutions. These intentional Eucharistic communities need to become the central important units of societal life, that is, to become fundamental social units within our modern culture for the humanization of all persons and social life.

The first difficulty, of course, is that we do not think of the Church as such communities. For most people the Church is one societal institution alongside others. Further we commonly think of Christian life from an individualistic or at best an organizational perspective. The essential nature of religious community is not easy to grasp on a continent where evangelists typically strive to win souls for Christ but rarely for Christ and his Church; where baptism is understood as a call to individual salvation rather than an incorporation into a family; where the Eucharist is seen as food for the individual soul rather than a communal thanksgiving meal; and where the Church is believed to be a voluntary association to which we individually belong by choice rather than a relationship into which God invites us, binding us together to be a sign and witness of God's reign in human history.

Insofar as some experience a disconnected, disintegrated, depersonalized society of autonomous individuals living competitively within a violent, estranged world, they image the Church as an intimate, closely knit, homogenous familial community in retreat from the world and public life. Such an idealized image is not only unrealizable, it encourages escapist behavior and thereby denies the Gospel's call to heterogeneity and agency for the transformation of culture.

As the Whiteheads point out in their book *Community of Faith,* we are ambivalent about community. On the one hand we desire communal life, and on the other hand we are committed to individualism. We want to share life and work, to be bound together by trust and compassion, but we remain committed to the autonomous pursuit of our own destiny and the rightful possession of what we have earned. We want the support that comes from belonging to a community of shared values, and yet we resent group restraints and binding ethical principles. We want a community that will make us feel at home in a bureaucratic world, but we are wary of group demands and expectations. We want the benefits of community without any of its responsibilities. We want the Church to replace the ethnic religious neighborhood and the extended family, so that we can have the benefits without any of the negatives inherent in those social structures. We want community but not what community demands. We may not like or find meaningful and satisfying our modern, impersonal, bureaucratic, competitive, individualistic, private society, but we are unwilling to give up what we count as its benefits in order to have a personal, familial, cooperative, communal, public society. We have become so enculturated into modernity that while acknowledging its dehumanizing character, we seem unable to free ourselves from its understandings and ways of life in order to find a more humane way to live.

Nevertheless it has been our contention that an intentional Eucharistic community is the best, the most meaningful image for faithfulness in the modern world. Having discussed its nature and character, we now turn to historical, theological, and liturgical issues.

References

Banks, Robert. *Paul's Idea of Community.* Grand Rapids: Eerdmans, 1980. An explanation of the early Christian house churches in their historical setting.

Bellah, Robert, *et al. Habits of Heart.* Berkeley: University of California Press, 1985. A social analysis of individualism and commitment in American life.

Bernard, Jesse. *The Sociology of Community.* Glenview, Ill.: Scott, Foresman, 1973. Discussion and critique of most of what we know about the sociology of community.

Best, James. *Another Way to Live.* Wellingford, Penn.: Pendle Hill, 1978. Experiencing intentional community.

Bouyer, Louis. *Rite and Man: Natural Sacredness of Christian Liturgy.* Notre Dame, Ind.: University of Notre Dame Press, 1963. An investigation of issues related to cultic and daily life, liturgy and everyday life.

Brown, Raymond. *The Community of the Beloved Disciple.* New York: Paulist Press 1979. A study of the Johannine Church in the first century.

Brueggemann, Walter. *The Prophetic Imagination.* Philadelphia: Fortress Press, 1978. An exploration of the Church as a community of alternative consciousness and perception to that of the dominant culture.

Chupungco, Anscar. *Cultural Adaptation of the Liturgy.* New York: Paulist Press, 1982. An exploration of liturgical change from a theological and cultural perspective.

Clark, David. *Basic Christian Communities.* Liverpool: Liverpool Institute of Socio-Religious Studies, 1978. Implications for Church and society.

Collins, Patrick. *More Than Meets the Eye.* New York: Paulist Press, 1983. Explores the renewal of liturgy as symbolic action and a form of art.

Delepesse, Max. *The Church Community.* Notre Dame, Ind.: Ave Maria Press, 1973. Exploration of intentional Catholic community in Europe and its implications for parish life and ministry.

Donavan, Vincent. *Christianity Rediscovered.* Notre Dame, Ind.: Fides/Claretian, 1978. Insights into the nature of Christian community and how each small intentional community can become "church."

Dulles, Avery. *Models of the Church.* Garden City, N.Y.: Doubleday 1974. An exploration of the basic functions of the Church and an assessment of its different roles toward the faithful and its mission on earth.

Grierson, Durham. *Transforming a People of God.* Melbourne: The Joint Board of Christian Education of Australia and New Zealand, 1984. An exploration of what forms, shapes, and sustains a faith community.

Holmes, Urban, and Westerhoff, John. *Christian Believing.* New York: Seabury, 1979. An exploration of the human religious quest and its healthy and sick manifestations.

Hug, James, ed. *Tracing the Spirit.* New York: Paulist Press, 1983. Theological reflection on the experience of small intentional communities engaged in the struggle for social justice.

Konig, Rene. *The Community.* New York: Schocken Books, 1968. An attempt to explain the meaning of the term community as a determinative system of social behavior.

Mariante, Benjamin. *Pluralistic Society, Pluralistic Church.* Washington: University Press of America, 1981. A sociological-theological exploration of the Church as a religious institution in the modern world and a defense of the Church as an intentional community.

Niebuhr, H. Richard. *Christ and Culture.* New York: Harper, 1951. An exploration of the various ways Christ or the Church can relate to culture.

Nisbet, Robert. *The Quest for Community.* New York: Oxford University Press, 1953. An exploration of the loss of community, its import on the lives of people, and their search for community.

Nisbet, Robert. *The Sociological Tradition.* New York: Basic Books, 1966.

Examines the use of community as a sociological category in the works of various social scientists.

O'Connor, Elizabeth. *The New Community.* New York: Harper & Row, 1976. The story of a community of faith and its relationship to society.

Palmer, Parker. *Company of Strangers.* New York: Crossroads, 1981. Christian community and the renewal of public life.

Reed, Bruce. *Dynamics of Religion.* London: Darton, Longman & Todd, 1978. The role of the Church and its worship in the human oscillation process between intradependence and extradependence.

Robinson, Edward. *The Original Vision.* New York: Seabury, 1983. A study of the religious experience of childhood and the Church.

Scherer, Jacqueline. *Contemporary Community.* New York: Harper & Row, 1973. Contemporary research in the experience of community in the structures of modern life including the parish.

Segundo, Juan Luis. *The Community Called Church.* Maryknoll, N.Y.: Orbis Books, 1968. A fresh vision of the Church and its relationship to the world.

Sennett, Richard. *The Fall of the Public Man.* New York: Vintage, 1978. Contemporary images of autonomy and community that influence American social life.

Shaughnessy, James, ed. *The Roots of Ritual.* Grand Rapids: Eerdmans, 1973. A collection of essays illustrating how persons in various disciplines view ritual with implications for liturgical reform.

Slater, Philip. *The Pursuit of Loneliness.* Boston: Beacon, 1970. Discussion of the tensions generated by contradictions in contemporary American experience.

Torres, Sergio, and Eagleson, John, eds. *The Challenge of Basic Christian Community.* Maryknoll, N.Y.: Orbis Books, 1981. Major papers of meeting of the Ecumenical Association of Third World Theologians on the Church as an intentional community.

Troeltch, Ernest. *Social Teachings of the Church.* New York: Macmillan, 1981. A social analysis of the Church.

Turner, Victor. *Dramas, Fields and Metaphors.* Ithaca N.Y.: Cornell University Press, 1974. An exploration of myth, symbol, and ritual from an anthropological perspective.

Westerhoff, John. *Building God's People.* New York: Seabury, 1983. A practical theology on what it means to live as a Christian in our day with special reference to liturgy.

Westerhoff, John. *Living a Faith Community.* Minneapolis: Winston/Seabury, 1985. An exploration of the nature and character of an intentional community of faith with special reference to liturgy.

Whitehead, Evelyn, and Whitehead, James. *Community of Faith.* New York: Seabury, 1982. Models and strategies for building Christian community.

Whitehead, Evelyn. *The Parish in Community and Ministry.* New York: Paulist Press, 1978. Parish community explored from a theological and social science perspective.

Wicker, Brian. *Culture and Liturgy.* New York: Sheed & Ward, 1963. An investigation of the relationships between liturgy, culture, and the social order.

Wilder, Amos. *Theopoetic.* Philadelphia: Fortress Press, 1976. An exploration of theology and the religious imagination with a focus on ritual symbols and myths.

2. THE EUCHARIST AND INTENTIONAL COMMUNITIES

John C. Haughey, S.J.

Introduction

Our volume is about the Eucharist looked at through the eyes of intentional communities. The North American Catholic Church has a growing number of intentional communities, but relative to our Third World brothers and sisters, we have very few such communities. Even where there are these few, we would have to ask ourselves how often they have come into existence because they are centered in the Eucharist. Yet the rhetoric surrounding Eucharist would lead one to believe that intentional communities would be the rule rather than the exception and that Eucharist would be the magnet and force that makes them more fervent, one, and effective in the world.

Being effective in the world has to be one of the intentionalities of intentional communities. They do not exist merely for themselves or their members. Like the Master they come into being that the world may know the one true God and him whom he has sent. I have been impressed recently by the coincidence between the experience of intentional communities and the lamentation of American economists. Any number of the studies about the American economy done in the last few years, especially those that seek to make it healthier and more just, cite an identifiable community and identification with it as critical both to economic justice and economic health. These analyses start from the givens of the present economic system and go from there to a more just and ideal form of production and distribution in the future. But getting from now to then always has to pass through the maze—even the mine fields—of the special interests. The power to deliver a more equitable economic future runs up against the seemingly intractable individualism that economy itself has been so instrumental in forming. Radical economic analyses, in other words, explicitly or implicitly, call for new persons, a change in anthropology, and a different sense of selfhood or identity. Modern anthropology, according to Pope John Paul II, is deeply flawed by what he calls "economism."[1] It is at the heart of most social impasses. By "economism" he means the reduction of the meaning of human dignity to economic categories such as consumption, production, and solvency. The American Catholic bishops in their pastoral letter "Economic Justice for All" rightly claim that "will" is what is lacking to bring about the radical changes American society must come to in order for the United States to develop the economic democracy their letter calls for.[2]

All of these factors account for the particular focus of this chapter on the Eucharist and intentional communities. That focus will be on a change in consciousness, moving from a consciousness that operates on a narrow horizon of self-interest to a consciousness that is, for want of a better word, communitarian. By communitarian consciousness I mean an awareness of membership in a social whole, one of several such wholes in fact. It is not that the subject whose consciousness is communitarian is oblivious of self. Such subjects see their own uniqueness in relationship to these social wholes rather than themselves as individuals who are only accidentally also connected to several communities.

The Catholic community has a resource that it largely neglects for the development of a communitarian consciousness. That resource, which I might add is at the center of its *praxis*, is Eucharist. But how can it be at the center of our *praxis*, and yet our experience is that there is very little communitarian consciousness? To pin our hopes for a change in consciousness on Eucharist seems to put our hopes on something that has not delivered, so to speak. Furthermore, if my analysis goes from the present Eucharistic givens to some ideal future in which many will walk about with a highly communitarian consciousness, do we not run into the same kind of impasse the economists run into, namely, the intractability of the myopic sense of self of the participants at the Eucharist? The answer would be certainly yes, if I thought Eucharist truly was being celebrated in our North American Church. The fact is that I believe that we have only barely begun to celebrate Eucharist. Where it is being celebrated, its concelebrants become communitarian people. This chapter, therefore, is not a recommendation that we add anything to Eucharist, but that we subtract from the manner of our celebration of it the dispositions or senses of self that we carry into it from our economically fueled culture. It is not that we have to become something we are not, but that we must allow God to complete in us what God has already begun. We are not allowing Eucharist to be itself. If we let the Lord nourish us, all our other suppers would feel the impress his supper left on us.

There is a way of using faith, of course, which if you put yourself in God's shoes, must be repugnant to God. It goes somewhat as follows. First, a problematic social situation is cited; hence a solution is needed. The faith is then employed to solve the problem in question. Since I might be accused of this kind of "solutionism," let me defend myself and explain further what this chapter will try to do. We do have a cultural problem described variously as excessive individualism, privatism, materialism, or "economism." The solution obviously is community. I am not trying to make the Eucharist the solution to the problem. I am saying that if Eucharist were truly Eucharist, the Church would be making an enormous contribution to solving the culture's problem.

Eucharist is not only ideally a statement to a culture; it is also itself an expression of the culture in which it is celebrated. The Westerhoff chapter describes some of the characteristics of our American culture. The Second Vatican Council was at pains to show how the Church was not to fight the culture within which the people of God existed, but was to alternately stimulate, advance, strengthen, perfect, and restore it.[3] This is no easy job. The most difficult aspect of it is the discernment of that which is to be strengthened and perfected and that which is to be critiqued and opposed. This chapter will seek to do this in some small way by making use of a Eucharistic paradigm as the instrument for this discerning. What will come from this, hopefully, is an understanding of Eucharist that will make the Eucharist a statement to our American culture that could affirm, strengthen, and perfect its positive qualities and heighten the consciousness at least of the concelebrants about what in their culture is congenial and what is inimical to their faith.

The most inimical feature of our culture, I believe, is its inability to bring its citizens beyond their narrowly construed interests.

Conversely, the most important contribution I believe the good news can bring to our American culture is its ability to form communitarian individuals. The Eucharist is the key to this formation. We need not, in fact must not, manipulate the Eucharist to produce social effects. But we need to free the Eucharist from the bonds within which it is celebrated, and then these social effects will be felt in the culture.

The Corinthian Eucharist

The paradigm I will use comes from the earliest New Testament text we have on the Eucharist. Fortunately it is exactly what the introduction indicated was needed, namely, a critical discernment of Eucharistic behavior so that the Eucharist would be free to bring forth its truth in the concelebrants. There is buried in this letter a theology of Eucharist that, I believe, must be unearthed for us to become excited again about the action of the Eucharist. It might be misleading, however, to call it a theology of Eucharist, since it was not at all Paul's intention to construct such a thing. But even his ad hoc comments are theologically more profound than most of our present insights into the Eucharist.

By paradigm I mean an exemplary event along with an interpretation of the phenomena that emerge from the event which are analogous to the phenomena we seek to interpret and which we take to be a valid reading of them. It has also been called a metatheory, a construct, or an exemplar.[4]

> The Lord's Supper. What I now have to say is not said in praise, because your meetings are not profitable but harmful. First of all, I hear that when you gather for a meeting there are divisions among you, and I am inclined to believe it. There may even have to be factions among you for the tried and true to stand out clearly. When you assemble it is not to eat the Lord's Supper, for everyone is in haste to eat his own supper. One person goes hungry while another gets drunk. Do you not have homes where you can eat and drink? Would you show contempt for the church of God, and embarrass those who have nothing? What can I say to you? Shall I praise you? Certainly not in this matter!
> I received from the Lord what I handed on to you, namely, that the Lord Jesus on the night in which he was betrayed took bread, and after he had given thanks, broke it and said, "This is my body, which is for you. Do this in remembrance of me." In the same way, after the supper, he took the cup, saying, "This cup is the new covenant in my blood. Do this, whenever you drink it, in remembrance

of me." Every time, then, you eat this bread and drink this cup, you proclaim the death of the Lord until he comes! This means that whoever eats the bread or drinks the cup of the Lord unworthily sins against the body and blood of the Lord. A man should examine himself first; only then should he eat of the bread and drink of the cup. He who eats and drinks without recognizing the body eats and drinks a judgment on himself. That is why many among you are sick and infirm, and why so many are dying. If we were to examine ourselves, we would not be falling under judgment in this way; but since it is the Lord who judges us, he chastens us to keep us from being condemned with the rest of the world. Therefore, my brothers, when you assemble for the meal, wait for one another. If anyone is hungry let him eat at home, so that your assembly may not deserve condemnation (1 Cor 11:17-34).

"Do this in remembrance of me" (1 Cor 11:24)—the command is to do the actions that respond to God's action and this makes the participants members of the body of his Son and members of one another. The Corinthian Christians were acting in a manner that was decidedly disobedient to the command. They were, of course, honoring and believing in Christ in their Eucharistic assemblies, but not in accordance with the way he wished to be believed in and praised. They had begun to construe their Christian faith and Christ himself in ways that conformed him to their unconverted hearts. It also left their culture unmolested. Paul, however, profoundly critiqued their accommodating spirit and sought to have them cease from reading their faith through their culture's blind eyes.[5] They had maneuvered their understanding of faith around to the point where they were now free to revert to their old prejudices and interests. Paul's attempt to reverse these dynamics and bring them back to a pristine understanding of their faith needs to be studied closely. There is a wrong way of going about celebrating the Eucharist—the way the Corinthians were doing it—and a right way, which was Paul's.

The Corinthian way makes several errors of judgment. Many Corinthians were prone to "gnosticize" their new faith, making it into something more of thought and knowledge than of life and action, something that worked internal changes that were not expected to surface into social transformations. As a result the effects on the body politic of the nascent Church of Corinth were negligible. The opposite, unfortunately, was not the case; the body politic had considerable effect on the Christians.

Still another error closely linked to the above was that the at-
tendees at the Eucharists at Corinth were, as Bornkamm put it,
"profaning the body of Christ precisely under the mask of an increasing sacralization of the Eucharistic food."[6] The elements of
bread and wine were being set over against the whole action and
its actors. The elements were being made the object of attention
and reverence, and behind this convenient move the Risen Christ
was being reverenced. This was a failure in discernment of the peculiar character of Christ as Paul preached him. For Paul, Christ
was inextricably the person of Christ-and-his-own-members. To fail
to see this, or to refuse to see, was to fail to recognize the body (see 1
Cor 11:29). The failure was more likely when the Corinthians believed that the total object of the celebration at their meal assemblies was the individuated person of Jesus. As a result, during and
after these assemblies, they felt free to retain many of the attitudes
and the behavior they had before Paul came to Corinth. They returned, therefore, from their Eucharistic assemblies to society under-
equipped to live in a Christian way, because they had not recognized
that they were eating and drinking a judgment on themselves (see
1 Cor 11:29). Had they recognized the body, their behavior during
and after the assemblies would have had to change.

Failure in will and desire was of a piece with the perceptual errors that accompanied them, so it is difficult to know which came
first. In either case the behavioral consequences were heart-breaking
to Paul. He was informed of the style of their assemblies at which
many refused fellowship beyond their own clans and economic or
social classes. Because they were divided into cliques or factions
(1 Cor 11:18-19), they were celebrating an action which said one
thing (one bread, one body, 1 Cor 10:17) but did another (Christ
was divided into parts, 1 Cor 1:13). Also those who had nothing,
probably because they were poor or were slaves who came late after
feeding their masters, were embarrassed (1 Cor 11:22).[7] In addition those who had plenty had too much to drink (1 Cor 11:21).
The very purpose for assembling together, therefore, was deeply
twisted, because although it was to eat the Lord's supper, most were
in great haste to eat their own (1 Cor 11:21).

The effect of their "contempt for the church of God" (1 Cor
11:22) or for this mystery of Christ-and-members also had considerable ramifications between Eucharists. Theirs was a vincible error
about the character of the Body of Christ, and consequently they
had eaten and drunk a judgment upon themselves (1 Cor 11:29).

What does Paul mean by this judgment? By baptism believers escaped the judgment of God. They were acquitted of all the sins of which they were guilty. Incorporation into the Christ mystery involves cleansing, propitiation, and atonement. As long as one chooses to live within this mystery, one is not subject to the judgment which can condemn. To be in Christ makes one at the present time and in this age a participant in the age to come where there is no condemnation. With baptism, furthermore, there is faith. By faith one is capable of making right judgments about Christ, oneself, and one's relationship to one another and the world.

Right judgments and their attendant actions keep one from falling back into the condition in which one would be judged by God.[8] Wrong judgments, on the other hand, can bring one back into that former condition. "If we were to examine ourselves [if we discerned the Body and the relationship we have to it and one another] we would not be falling under judgment" (1 Cor 11:31). Paul exhorts his colleagues to right self-judgment or to a reexamination of themselves lest they fall under judgment. Their sin was not a lack of faith in Jesus; it was an erroneous judgment. They were in error about who they were, because they were wrong about who he was now. Their belief was in a disembodied Jesus. They believed in one not embodied the way he said he would be and Paul said he was. They were also in error about the character of the Last Supper. Paul was seeking to correct their Christology by plunging their actions at the Eucharist back into the account of the institution of the Eucharist that had been handed on to him.[9]

For the error to be seen, it had to be felt by its effects. Immediately after warning them that "He who eats and drinks without recognizing the body eats and drinks a judgment on himself," Paul notes that "many among you are sick and infirm . . . and are dying" (1 Cor 11:29-30). He is alleging that sinful or antisocial or nonmember behavior towards one another has physical effects in the whole body. To act nonorganically has physical consequences on individuals—weakness, illness, and death. According to his anthropology, in the old creation death reigned.[10] Not to be truly incorporated into the new creation and the Eucharist community made one prey to all the evils that affected those who lived in the reign in which death still held sway.

While people escaped judgment by being suffused with the righteousness won for them by Christ, nevertheless, this victory could be overdone. Consequently many of the Corinthians were immaturely imagining themselves to be in a condition of exaltation which was simply untrue and unreal. Their "theology of glory" enabled them to distance themselves from the sacrifice of the Cross by reason of which and in which they were baptized. Concretely they were embracing a faith that cost them little and had little social effect. Paul argues "Every time, then, you eat this bread and drink this cup, you proclaim the death of the Lord until he comes" (1 Cor 11:26). His choice of words gives a further proof that Paul was anxious to root out the antisomatic, gnostic tendencies which were disintegrating the corporate consciousness he had hoped to inculcate in the Corinthian Christians. Notice the words in this verse: "Your Eucharists proclaim his death until he comes." Paul was anxious to emphasize they were *between* two moments, the first one being when the Lord gave himself up in death and the second the coming of the Lord in the future. These words are significant because they are contrary to a "fanatical transcending of the boundaries of time in a spiritual-eschatological enthusiasm."[11] Those who had enthused and theologized themselves into a theology of glory proclaimed the Lord's and their own resurrection as something now. In their state of spiritual euphoria, they were inducing a triumphalistic degree of glory. Instead Paul roots their celebrations within time and history and their relations with one another.

Corinth was notorious throughout the entire Mediterranean world for its ethnic antipathies, its exploitation of women, its rapaciousness, and its catastrophic economic inequalities.[12] It was a symbol of what Paul called the works of the flesh. From the flesh according to Paul, proceed "hostilities, bickering, jealousy, outbursts of rage, selfish rivalries, dissensions, factions, envy, drunkenness, orgies, and the like" (Gal 5:20). But to his dismay these were the very qualities that were beginning to appear in the social behavior of the Christian Corinthians. The old creation was determining the new creation. In the old systems there were divisions and isolates, for example, "Jew or Greek, slave or freeman, male or female." This would not be in the new creation, for "all are one in Christ Jesus" (Gal 3:28).

When informed of the pattern of behavior that had developed at Corinthian Eucharistic celebrations, the Apostle to the Gentiles was appalled because what God had joined together, namely God's Son and those who believed in him, people had pulled apart. Paul's admonition in 1 Cor 11 addresses the indissolubility of the union between head and members. Their behavior toward one another indicated that the participants themselves had not grasped the fact, the intimacy, or the import of this union. The superficiality of their conversion was evident. Their belief in Christ was unmistakable, but in their behavior toward one another, they made it clear that they could not have believed that each of them was a member, an inviolable, unique, sacred instance of the Christ reality. If they had, they would have seen that their behavior toward one another was sacrilegious.

Paul looked upon Eucharistic assemblies with an imagination permeated with the power of faith. Those whose imaginations refused to be so fired saw in these Eucharistic assemblies only acts of worship of God in Christ. Paul went much further and saw these moments as times when many individuals were being further joined to one another in a single reality that was both personal and social, hence a "new man." In the process individuals were to become communitarian in fact. To see people, along with oneself, as members of a whole or as members of one another meant that a communitarian consciousness would come to be in the Christian community.

If the local communities that were being drawn into the Christ mystery lived out the baptism and the Eucharist, they would be the empirical and tangible evidence to nonbelievers that Christ still existed and that belief in him was an alternative to what they had known life to be. But the mission would fail if the whole reality of the Christ presence was not being appropriated. And it was not being appropriated, because only part of the mystery was believed. *He* was believed in, but not according to the manner in which he was present, namely, as head conjoined to members.

The Form of the Mystery

There are two Pauline master images which can elucidate the form of Christ that God would bring into being. The one is body/soma; the other is fellowship/*koinonia*. Paul's favorite expression for describing the social wholeness he observed and experienced in Christian communities is Christ's Body. Jesus was really becoming Lord of individuals, and individuals in turn were really changing their relationship to the other individuals who also confessed Jesus as their Lord. The change had to be named. It showed itself in innumerable, concrete acts of interdependence and mutuality. While these were very tangible, simple human actions, at the same time Paul does not think the degree of intimacy that he finds between those performing those actions can be explained by merely human affection or effort. They are expressing and creating more than a human bonding. He sees them all as so many moments of upbuilding a reality that is more than the sum total of all the parts. He sees nothing less than Christ's own presence being built up through the favor each one receives from God. Before it was a doctrine to be assented to, it had to be an experience looking for a name. The name Paul found was "Body." The communities were Christ's Body. They were members of his reality and members of one another as a result.

This experiential discovery of the fact that the Lord was knitting together people as intimately as if they were so many members of his Son's own Body took several years to mature. It is not until this letter to the Corinthians we are examining here (probably between 53 and 55 A.D.) that Paul uses such an expression.[13] By then he sees the aptness of such a bold expression. It should be noted, too, that by then he was aware of the implications for "the body politic" if "the body Christian" were to fail in achieving the relational wholeness it was capable of growing into. Were that to happen, the mission of the communities to the culture would grind to a halt.

Individuals knitted together in a bonding so close as to be like a single body with many differences would be evidence that a new kind of city was possible, something other than the fragmentation Corinth had known. The knitting together of individuals would be their redemption and at the same time would be the beginning of the recapitulation of all in Corinth who saw and wanted this alternative.

The doctrine of the Body of Christ does not have the impact today that it had on the first generations of Christianity, partly because it suffers from having been flattened out or "ecclesiologized." We have come to believe that we are in some ecclesial sense Christ's Body, but Paul is saying something much more profound than this. In 1 Corinthians 12:12 he is saying that just as a body is one with many members and all the members of a body, though many, are one body, *this is who Christ is now.*[14] This must be heard as a Christological statement for it to impact the hearer. Paul meant it to be a Christological statement. What he is saying is not only that the many are one, but that the one the many are is Christ. He is saying more than that individuals participate in Christ or that through baptism they are made part of an ecclesial reality. He is saying that together they are Christ. He is saying that in addition to being Lord of the universe, Christ Jesus is also an immanent reality in Corinth. He is saying something more than that individuals belong to the Church or even that they belong to Christ's Body; he is saying that many individuals together are so conjoined to the Risen Lord that he and they are the Christ now.[15]

The point Paul makes by naming the experience of Christian communities in this way is so basic that it is more often than not softened so that it is not allowed to say what in fact it means. In addition to "ecclesiologizing" it, one of our favorite ways of dulling the impact of calling these Christian communities Christ is to begin to distinguish the relationship between Christ and the members of his Body in terms like ontological, moral, functional, and other such distinctions that Paul himself would not have conceived. Paul knew as well as anyone that there was not a total identification between the uncreated and the created, between the divine and the human, between the people of God and their Savior and Lord. His letters abound with acknowledgement of that. Hence the bride is distinguishable from the bridegroom, the field from the planter, the pot from the potter, and so on. But distinctions have hardened into separations. Hence incarnation speaks of his reality not ours. The Body of Christ comes to be seen as something more like an appendage trailing the Risen Lord from a distance. But for Paul the meaning of body connotes the whole of the person, the person acting, the person choosing—the living person.[16]

How could a statement like 1 Cor 12:12 make sense? As if anticipating the question Paul answers it in the very next verse: "For by one Spirit we are all baptized into one body—Jews or Greeks, slaves or free—and all were made to drink of one Spirit" (1 Cor 12:13). Paul brings together the four ingredients, so to speak, that are necessary in order to explain the remarkable assertion he has made in the preceding verse. These four ingredients—the Spirit, baptism, Body, and Eucharist—elucidate one or another aspect of the mystery. Of these four the Spirit is the key ingredient. Once the Holy Spirit is introduced, the transcendent and immanent can be conjoined, because the Spirit traverses the depths of each (Rom 8:26-27). The Spirit can also knit the divine and human together into a single personality.[17] In both the incarnation and the presence of this Christ-presence in Corinth *cum* members, the explanation of the indissoluble unity between the one and the many is ascribed to the Spirit.

When Jesus died, the same thing happened to him as happens in any human death: his body and his human spirit underwent some kind of a separation. Unlike any other human death, however, Jesus came into a new relationship with his Body. Looked at from his side, he was raised; looked at from our side, his own Body became the created means through which his spirit was dispensed to other human beings. Before his death, as is the case with any human being, his Spirit touched the world through his Body. Now his Spirit would touch the universe through his Body. Before his death the expressions of his personality were tied to the principle of limitation, which is matter. Now his Body is not limited by matter, as is true of "a body of death," but the whole of the material universe is "at the service of his manifestation."[18] The Eucharist and baptism are key in this. Through baptism Christ's own death and resurrection can now become definitional of individuals, more definitional than their own births and deaths. Individuals, furthermore, who are so baptized and nourished on the Christ mystery at the Eucharist become definitional of who Christ is now.

Paul offers more insight into the Eucharist and our participation in the Christ mystery through the master image of *koinonia* or fellowship with Christ and one another. Paul did not invent the word *koinonia*. In its previous history it was used by Greek philosophy to describe a degree of friendship between two or more people so intense that it included the mutual sharing of material goods.[19] Qumran also used the word to convey the notion of the surrender of property by the community's members to the community so that by rule members did not own anything of their own.[20] In the New Testament it was used by Paul, John, and Luke. In 1 John 1:3 the author explains that the purpose of his writing is "so that you may share [*koinonia*] life with us. This fellowship [*koinonia*] of ours is with the Father and with his son, Jesus Christ." Here *koinonia* conveys the communion of Father with Son in the Godhead into which the writer and his brothers and sisters are brought.

In Luke *koinonia* is used to describe the community after Pentecost. It is said to be devoted "to the apostles' instruction and the communal life" [*koinonia*] (Acts 2:42). Its cognate is *koina*, things-in-common.[21] "Those who believed shared all things in common" (Acts 2:44). Their communality, their *koinonia*, included a sharing of goods as a way of relating to one another.

At the hands of Luke, John, and Paul, *koinonia* implicitly begins to be a description of the inner reality of Trinity, long before Trinity is even thought of as a description of the divine mystery. These New Testament writers give us the beginnings of Trinity. Hence *koinonia* or communion is what the Father had with the Son, the Son with the Father, and the Spirit with the Father and the Son.

We will limit ourselves to Paul's notion, because it should elucidate the text on which we have concentrated our attention. Pauline *koinonia* includes the heights and the pits of human reality. For example Paul greets the Corinthian Christians with the prayer and wish: "The grace of the Lord Jesus Christ, and the love of God, and the fellowship [*koinonia*] of the Holy Spirit be with you all" (2 Cor 13:13). Their communion with one another is something Father, Son, and Spirit share with those who have been called into it. Not only are the faithful capable of being brought into *koinonia* in the Holy Spirit but also in the Son. "God is faithful, and it was he who called you to fellowship [*koinonia*] with his Son" (1 Cor 1:9). *Koinonia* takes place because God initiates a bonding between his Son and believers.

While the term refers to the internal life of God, it broadens in Paul's writings to include communion with and sharing in human needs and sufferings. The experience of Christ he already had only deepened his yearning "to know Christ and the power flowing from his resurrection" and "to know how to share [*koinonia*] in his sufferings by being formed into the pattern of his death" (Phil 3:10). Paul sees an unbroken continuity between the action of God which gives us a share in the risen life of Jesus and a share in his sufferings. *Koinonia* is used in both of these participations or entries. The present form of Christ in time, in other words, is both communion with Christ risen and communion here and now with his suffering. I wish . . . to know how to share in his sufferings" (Phil 3:10). The Risen Lord cannot be the one referred to here, since he has already suffered. Yet the suffering referred to here is both his and present suffering. Recall that Paul's introduction to Jesus was of one who presented himself in this manner from the outset: " 'Saul, Saul why do you persecute me?' 'Who are you, sir?' he asked. The voice answered, 'I am Jesus, the one you are persecuting' " (Acts 9:4-5). Jesus then was suffering in his members at Saul's hands. Now Paul, who suffered shipwreck and famine and scourging and every kind of affliction for Jesus, was still anxious from his prison cell to know how he could have an even greater share in and a deeper participation in this one Christ, both through the power of the resurrection flowing into him and through the community which by its members' sufferings were being transformed along with Paul into the pattern of his death.

Paul poured out his life like a libation for the sake of the community in this *koinonia* (Phil 2:17). When one member was honored, they all were, according to his communitarian consciousness. And when one member suffered, they all suffered. Because they were all in it together, he exhorted all members not to seek their own interest but rather that of their neighbor (see 1 Cor 10:24). In this they would imitate Paul as he imitates Christ: "As I try to please all in any way I can by seeking, not my own advantage, but that of the many. . . ." (1 Cor 10:33).

They are to be concerned to meet the concrete material needs of others with a special attention to those who have been brought together in Christ. Consequently collections are taken "on the first day of each week . . . whatever he has been able to save" (1 Cor 16:2). These are "for the saints" (1 Cor 16:1). But also from one part of the new Body of Christ, another part of that Body is supplied. To be particular, from communities in Macedonia and Corinth, the needy Jerusalem community is sustained. Paul informs the Corinthians that the Macedonian Christians, upon hearing of the needs in Jerusalem, gave "beyond their means," having "begged us insistently for the favor of sharing in this service to members of the church" (2 Cor 8:3-4). *Koinonia* is grounded in *diakonia*. *Diakonia* is serving the *koinonia*, pouring out one's life and sharing one's goods for the sake of the social whole that God is bringing together in the Spirit through the Son. Paul here meshes the two notions of *koinonia* and *diakonia* into a single phrase.

The character of Christian life takes its cue from the life it has received, the life it participates in in the Eucharist. "Is not the cup of blessing we bless a sharing in [*koinonia*] the blood of Christ?" (1 Cor 10:16). This Blood was poured out for the many. To drink of this cup creates an allegiance with the person of Christ that makes some loyalties impossible and all others secondary to this primary loyalty. It furthermore bonds those people, whose primary allegiance is to Christ, to one another in a bond so close that they have the same life-force pulsing through them.

"And is not the bread we break a sharing in [*koinonia*] the body of Christ?" (1 Cor 10:16)—again the rich levels of meaning, one not excluding the other. The body here is the Lord's own Body and therefore the correlate of his Blood. But it is also the body comprised of people members. But the main concern of Paul here is to stake out the identity or the social boundaries that are created by participation in the Blood and the Body of Christ. "Because the loaf of bread is one, we, many though we are, are one body, for we all partake of the one loaf" (1 Cor 10:17).

In effect he is saying: God is forging something new while we are asked to come into a consciousness about what that is. Becoming one with him and becoming one with one another are the two meanings of the one action. We are now members of an Us! The bread we break is one bread. We break it with and for one another. Because it is what it is, we know that we are called to be bread for one another. "Do this in remembrance of me" (1 Cor 11:4). There is considerable significance in the fact that the bread that is eaten is broken and yet from one loaf. We are drawn into the *koinonia* that is the life of the Trinity. Its extension into history is *diakonia*. The communitarian consciousness comes to see what God is doing in Christ. All of these are the fruit of the Eucharist that is done in remembrance of him.

Being Love

Paul's insight into the mystery of Jesus reaches even greater depth in his meditation in 1 Cor 13. He was sure that what was still wanting in the Corinthian assemblies and in the Body of Christ was love. Love is the gift that is received at the Eucharist. Love is the field of force Christians are brought into. It is not first and foremost a moral principle nor a virtue that inheres in the soul of Christians.[22] It begins outside of time but enters it, and Christians are able to enter into and abide in it. Hence love is a new way of being and acting that supercedes all previous ways. "I will show you the way which surpasses all the others" (1 Cor 13:1).

Paul interestingly does not exhort the Corinthians to conduct themselves one way or another. I presume the reason for this is that he believes that this love is a gift. Set your heart on it, therefore, is his exhortation; not: be this way or that! (see 1 Cor 12:31). Seek eagerly after it! (see 1 Cor 14:1). He is content, then, to describe it by its effects in those who receive it. Love brings a certain character to ordinary activity. The social wholeness that is described by the terms *koinonia* or body will materialize only through those who abide in love. Where there is patience and kindness, it will flourish. Where there is boasting, arrogance, or jealousy, social wholeness is unlikely, and so forth. This love is a new way of being and a new way of being with one another. It does not usually call for different actions. It calls for ordinary human activity done in a different way. It does not separate people from history, their humanity, their relationships, nor the activities human beings commonly do and have to do. Love enables those receiving and abiding in it to know and achieve instances of social wholeness. It does not, however, furnish them with a societal form they have to construct that is extrinsic to their own humanity.

Paul is not describing the ideal conduct of the Christian in this whole passage. He is describing "the love of God that comes to us in Christ Jesus, our Lord" (Rom 8:39). This love commits itself to us in such a way that from God's side at least, "neither death nor life, neither angels nor principalities, neither the present nor the future, nor powers, neither height nor depth nor any other creature will be able to separate us" from this love (Rom 8:38-39). Bornkamm astutely observes that "every understanding of love as virtue and deed turns the gospel of 1 Cor 13 into law, in that it directs itself to the striving and duty of man instead of . . . what God has done."[23]

This love should be most evident when the members come together in worship, as Paul rightly assumes. This is why he is so testy about evidence to the contrary. Liturgies were to be power moments, occasions which gave the strongest evidence of this love. This love was both given at that time and sensed at that time in an experience of transcendence.

It is easy to love the lovable and difficult to love the unlovable. A person's lovability is contingent on their being differentiated from the social wholes of which they are a part. Individuation is what love foments just as certainly as it does unity and communion. The uniqueness of each of the members of the Body of Christ will develop where there is love. This uniqueness will be of a different sort, however, than the individuality that develops when there is no love. The latter develops for the self, the former for the community, to build up the Body to contribute to the common good. The one differentiation takes place in isolation, apart from community and despite those with whom individuals have natural bonds. It separates and distances. The other differentiation takes place in, through, and with community. The resultant uniqueness is for community, for its upbuilding, for the enrichment of the many.

I believe all of this is implied in Paul's notion of the charisms. The charisms are the evidence of the differentiation of the members. The charisms are the way individuals build up the social whole. The primary charism, the gift of the Spirit that is foundational to the well-being and growth of the Body, is love. Love is what makes the Body and each of its members lovable. Love is what makes each of the members live for one another and for the many God would draw to the divine through the existential reality of the presence of the Body. Love is what makes the secondary charisms develop, and love of one another is what the exercise of all the charisms should lead to. Without love the exercise of the gifts becomes disorderly, as Paul shows so well in 1 Cor 14. Again this becomes evident when they assemble for the form of Eucharistic prayer that was extant in the early years.

If the members were rooted in love, then the exercise of the gifts of each of the members would be constructive (see 1 Cor 14:26). Together they would be building with and in and through these gifts. The metaphor of constructing a building is apt. "We are God's co-workers . . . his building" (1 Cor 3:9). Care is to be exercised as each adds to the foundation that had been laid. "Different ones build on this foundation" (see 1 Cor 3:12) (which is Jesus Christ) with the materials they bring to its construction (see 1 Cor 3:10-12). The motif of the edification of the congregation into the Body of Christ, or the temple of God, or the koinonia of God's people-with-God unifies the many subjects in 1 Corinthians and acts as the single criterion Paul uses to critique the behavior of their problem members.[24]

There are three groups of Christians in the Corinthian Church whose failures were love failures, hence their consciousness was not communitarian. One of these groups was composed of those who had succumbed to a gnosticized Christianity. They were careless about the members. They acted like they were beyond history, having already arrived at the consummation Paul was only expecting.[25] They mistook their own induced enthusiasm for the completion of the kingdom. The unloving ways in which they exercised their spiritual gifts was the tip-off to Paul. They were interested in having their own spiritual highs. Otherwise they would have conducted themselves in a more edifying way, a way which would be upbuilding of one another with a consciousness that was aware of their impact on others. Paul rejects an individualism that uses a false understanding of spirituality and exhausts itself in the production of spiritual phenomena in order to center upon itself.[26] To speak in angelic tongues or to prophesy with full knowledge of the mysteries without doing so from love gains nothing, is nothing, means nothing.

The other two groups were loose, if not in action at least in attitude, especially towards fornication and idol worship. Paul's comments on these two deepen our understanding of how a communitarian consciousness perceives this new, socially constituted Christ reality that was experiencing such growing pains in Corinth. One of the most severe growing pains was a boundaries one. Some of the converts to Christianity were Jewish, and some of the converts were Gentiles. Most of these latter would have participated formerly in the worship of idols. Converts from both groups would still be in contact with their former colleagues, friends and possibly family members. Paul exercises an ingenious series of discernments, the very number of which can be confusing if they are not aerated one by one. Each of his discernments brings out into clearer relief the basic criterion that is used by a communitarian consciousness.

The *koinonia* of Jesus-and-members has to see through two of the rationalizations by which many misjudged it. The rationalization process in both instances begins with the premise: "Everything is lawful for me" now that I am in Christ (1 Cor 6:12). Not so, Paul says, since being in Christ makes you a member of his Body. You are not free, for example, to take what is now Christ's and a member of Christ's Body and join it to a prostitute's body. This blunt imagery says much about Paul's material, physical, and social understanding of the Body of Christ that he saw himself and every other Christian transformed into. Notice that he is not propelled to articulate a sexual ethics under the provocation of the lewd conduct of some of the members. He is, however, provoked to insist on the new thing they are in Christ. The called for sexual conduct of the members must follow directly from what they have been made and become. A sexual ethics for Christians as a special discipline which is elaborated from reason or rational analysis is not Pauline in inspiration.

It is possible that these false notions of freedom came from the gnostic Christians, since they convey at least an implicit anthropology, one that dualized personality. Thus they saw their spirits as united to the Lord, but not their bodily selves. As a result they could exercise a freedom with their bodies, since these were not under the Lord. Consequently in matters of food or sex, they could do pretty much as they liked since our bodies will pass away (see 1 Cor 6:13). On the contrary, Paul insists. Bodies and spirits are united to Christ: "The body is not for immorality; it is for the Lord" (1 Cor 6:13). Nor is it passing away. God who raised up the Son, Body and Spirit, will also raise up the whole us (see 1 Cor 6:14). So "whoever is joined to the Lord becomes one spirit with him" (1 Cor 6:17). Furthermore "know that your body is a temple of the Holy Spirit, who is within" (1 Cor 6:19). Since, therefore, their bodily persons and their spirits were inextricable one from the other, Paul denies that their opportunistic dualizing is an authentic understanding of themselves or what God would do in them. What they must know about themselves and their freedom, he concludes, is that "You are not your own" (1 Cor 6:19). He underpins this principle with two salient facts, their baptisms and the sacrifice of Christ. "You have been purchased, and at a price." Consequently you are to "glorify God in your body" (1 Cor 6:20), that is with your whole person. Therefore "shun lewd conduct" since it does not bear witness to the action God does in you and through God's son (1 Cor 6:18).

The Communitarian Consciousness

The communitarian consciousness is not a sectarian one, as the following chapter of the letter (1 Cor 7) shows. The Jewish Christians sought to tighten up the Christian community in ways Paul found purist, conservative, and sectarian. A case in point was Christians who were married. Where only one partner of a marriage was Christian, Paul counseled against the separation of spouses, since the unbelieving spouse was consecrated by the believing spouse (see 1 Cor 7:14). But if the relationship between the two spouses was such that the unbelieving spouse was not willing to live with the spouse who has become a believer, then Paul allowed a separation since "God has called you to live in peace" (1 Cor 7:15). The Christian was not to be jeopardized in his or her living out of the Christ mystery because of any constraints imposed on them by the unbeliever's desire to separate him or her from the Body. But the believer was also to be alert to the fact that God might intend to sanctify the nonbeliever in and through the marriage. From the source of the holiness and wholeness of the believer, the unbeliever could experience the effects of God's presence and an existential call to salvation.[27]

Paul was sternly resisting the sectarian impulse of presumably Jewish Christians to cordon off the believers from the rest of the world. He had already ridiculed the idea that one could live in a world wholly disassociated from all immoral persons. "To avoid them, you would have to leave the world!" (1 Cor 5:10). But here he added a further rule of thumb: "Each one [believer] should lead the life the Lord has assigned him, continuing as he was when the Lord called him" (1 Cor 7:17). Paul's confidence is in the power of the Christ mystery. He would gradually destroy "every sovereignty, authority, and power" (1 Cor 15:24). Through his chosen ones he would "reign until God put all enemies under his feet" (1 Cor 15:25).

Hence his judgments disclose several important perceptions. The Christ mystery can take care of itself; it does not have to flee the civil community. Not only can it take care of itself, but it is meant to act as a source of consecration of that community. Members of the Body consecrate those who are not, such is the powerful influence of the holiness of the Body. This is not an exhortation; it is a description of the power that Paul expects to irradiate from the Body, signaling to those beyond the fellowship the alternative way of life Christians had discovered. But if there is a rejection of the believing spouse's response to be a member of the Body of Christ, the bond forged by marriage cedes to the bond forged by membership in Christ. "If the unbeliever wishes to separate, however, [because they cannot accept what the believing spouse has become] let him do so." For the same reason "the believing husband or wife is not bound in such cases" (1 Cor 7:15).

But these marriages were much less of a problem in the discernment of the relationship of the Christ mystery to non-Christian Corinth than the omnipresent issue of meats sacrificed to idols. Confusion and mistaken judgments were rife in the Christian community on this matter. There were two schools of thought operating, both of which Paul rejected. In the course of discerning what is called for, Paul articulates, as if they were asides, some invaluable insights into the communitarian consciousness, the value of which continues long after the issue of the sacrificed meats has ceased to bother anyone.

Of the two schools one was composed of Jewish Christians who were black and white about the matter: do not eat the stuff! (Acts 15:29). The other school, the gnosticized, in effect said: do not worry about it, because in Christ we now know that: "all things are lawful" (1 Cor 10:23); "the earth and its fullness are the Lord's" (1 Cor 10:26); and "we know that an idol is really nothing and that there is no God but one" (1 Cor 8:4). Paul forges a third way which is ingenious for its ability to account for all aspects of the question from within his unitary vision.

A word must first be said about the meat in question. Meat was not a normal part of the diet of the people of Corinth.[28] When it was available, it seems it had usually been slaughtered and sacrificed to the gods, according to one scholar. What came to the markets, "seems to have originated at sacrificial offerings."[29] Others are less sure of this: "The extent to which the Christian shopping in the Corinthian markets would be forced to purchase goods with a 're-ligious history' behind them must not be exaggerated."[30] We do not really have to choose between these two, since enough of the meat had a "religious history" to it to prompt the dilemma.

There were several options that were the subject of controversy. Could the meat be purchased? Paul counseled: "Eat whatever is sold in the market without raising any question of conscience" (1 Cor 10:25) because "the earth and its fullness are the Lord's" (1 Cor 10:26). This is the Pauline largesse of spirit that enjoys the free-dom by which Christ sets his own free. Why not since "all these [things] are yours" (1 Cor 3:22)? Paul shows the same freedom that Jesus showed, a freedom about which the Pharisees registered major complaints (see Mark 2:23ff). Paul's freedom, however, differed from the freedom of those who were careless about freedom in Christ. While "all these [things] are yours," you are not your own, "you are Christ's, and Christ is God's" (1 Cor 3:23). This person who is free is not free to define his or her personhood in terms of self. This person is free in Christ and because of Christ. Freedom is defined by inclusion in this mystery, not by an autonomy that imagines itself disengaged from it.

A second possibility arises: Christians are invited to dine with unbelievers. Paul seems to have the same open-ended attitude in this case as he had with respect to marriage with an unbeliever. "If an unbeliever invites you to his table and you want to go, eat whatever is placed before you, without raising any question of con-science" (1 Cor 10:27). Paul's sense of the relationship between the pagan culture and Christian faith is not a niggardly, sectarian one as we have seen.

But a wrinkle develops! Suppose someone raises an objection: "This [meat] was offered in idol worship" (1 Cor 10:28). Paul is quite clear: "Do not eat it, both for the sake of the one who called attention to it and on account of the conscience issue—not your own conscience but your neighbor's" (1 Cor 10:28-29). Why? First of all because of the importance of the bonds between you and the other members of the Body (or the potential members who could also have raised the question). In effect Paul says: "The bond between you is more important to preserve than the freedom and knowledge you might have personally arrived at in your conscience about the nontheological character of idol meat. Your knowledge in this case is right, but others would not have had the same opportunity or time to mature in the Christian community. In that case love requires that you not act on it." But an objection is raised to this: "Should my liberty be restricted by another man's conscience?" (1 Cor 10:29). It should, Paul contends. Why?

Recall Paul's assessment about knowledge and the effect it can have: " 'Knowledge' inflates, love upbuilds" (1 Cor 8:1). There is knowledge and knowledge. There is a knowing that can be right in itself (this is the case here since Paul agreed that since "an idol is really nothing, and . . . there is no God but one" [1 Cor 8:4], the meat is unaffected) but wrong in the ethos in which it is located. That wrong ethos is where love is wanting. The Pauline logic is tight here: "If a man thinks he knows something [and uses his knowledge for himself or to build himself up or uses it haughtily], that means he has never really known it as he ought. But if anyone loves God, that man is known by him" (1 Cor 8:2-3). Being known by God is what knowledge is for and leads to! Our knowledge, right as it may be about a particular issue, can be wrongly used if it is not exercised out of love, that is, with an eye to the good of one who is in Christ or who might be. Furthermore one must always be aware that: "My knowledge is imperfect now" (1 Cor 13:12). The perfection of knowledge goes in this direction: the one possessing it imperfectly will be possessed by love; it does not go in the direction of the one possessing it, possessing it perfectly. The formal object of the beatific vision is not the comprehension but the incomprehensibility of God.[31]

Furthermore, it is love that should govern knowledge. Love unites; therefore one takes into account the neighbor's conscience and not merely one's own knowledge and conscience. A loving Christian, in brief, will refuse to become an occasion of scandal or sin in those who, for whatever reason, do not yet possess an adequate theological understanding of meat sacrificed to idols (see 1 Cor 8:7-13).

But there is an even more interesting situation posed by Paul which prompts his most trenchant comments. It is the third possibility, as Paul sees it, about the question of food offered to idols. The Christian is invited to a meal that takes place in a religious establishment or temple at the table of a god at which a meal is offered to idols or at least that which had been previously sacrificed is the fare offered to the invitees (see 1 Cor 10:20). Here Paul's advice is not concerned with the conscience of the weak onlooker or even with the character of the meat but with the formally religious (pagan) character of the setting. It is too closely linked for him with the worship of alien gods. Therefore, "I am telling you, whom I love, to shun the worship of idols" (1 Cor 10:14).

Paul's advice is that they reject this kind of invitation for two reasons. One had to do with the nature of the place which was for worship of idols. The second reason was the character of their Christian worship. About the worship of idols: although "an idol is really nothing" (1 Cor 8:4), the worship of them generates a field of force, inimical to and at war with the *koinonia* the Christians had been brought into. Paul, therefore, can simultaneously believe that idols are nothing and yet observe that "there are many such 'gods' and 'lords'" (1 Cor 8:5). The very worship makes them gods and lords because they are being invested with a power they would not otherwise have. Elsewhere Paul observes this dynamic: "when you offer yourself to someone as obedient slaves, you are the slaves of the one you obey" (Rom 6:16).

Although idols are nothing, evidently not so "demons," according to Paul. These seem to have some kind of reality independent of the worshiper in Paul's eyes. They can exert an influence— although again their influence materializes when people enter into some form of relationship to them by seeming to pay them homage or acknowledging their power, for example, here by being participants at their table (see 1 Cor 10:21). Paul, therefore, seems to make a distinction in 1 Cor 10:19-20 "between gods worshiped by means of idols and (demons), i.e., evil forces at work in paganism that may even have a relationship to the gods that, as such, are non-existent."[32] If Christians go to the temple and join in some way in the services there, they in effect "become sharers with demons" (1 Cor 10:20). In effect what he says is this: you can be in relationship with your pagan neighbors and their culture, but you cannot enter into the fields of force or the allegiances to which they are tethered. But you do so by being partners with your neighbors at their altars and temple tables when these allegiances, these loyalties, are affirmed.

The Eucharist forged a wholly different and radical allegiance. The Eucharistic table was the place where their primary allegiance was affirmed and promised. "Is not the cup of blessing we bless a sharing in [koinonia] the blood of Christ?" (1 Cor 10:16). Therefore any alienation of our bonds, any straying from this our primal allegiance, constitute not only a betrayal of the Lord but also of the community. The Eucharist has been a partaking of one loaf, and a participation of many in the one Body (see 1 Cor 10:17).

"Partaking of the Lord's Supper does not first and foremost serve the edification of the individual, but unites the individuals to form the body of Christ."[33] Therefore "you cannot partake of the table of the Lord and likewise the table of demons" (1 Cor 10:21). We must be true to who we are and to what we have done! We have one Lord, and we should do all for his glory (see 1 Cor 10:31). Neither should we provoke him to jealous anger (see 1 Cor 10:22) nor give offense to believers and nonbelievers alike by self-interested behavior (see 1 Cor 10:24). The norm of action, therefore, that follows immediately from the action done to us and by us at the Eucharist is: "do what builds up and confirm what you have celebrated and been made." "All things are lawful" (1 Cor 10:23) but everything is not for the best. What is for the best is what builds the *koinonia*, and not everything does.

The Boundaries

Some further reflection on Eucharistic *praxis* is called for here. Every Eucharist is a statement to at least the concelebrants about power and identity. The statement can be overstated, understated, or misstated. I would judge it an overstatement when there is no correspondence between the evidence and the alleged experience of union with God, especially as a result of the celebration of the sacrament. These experiences of union with God are much more measurable than we are ordinarily willing to admit. If the measurement of this union is done according to the way God has revealed self to us, it will have social, communal evidence to ground it. The proof of this contention runs throughout Scripture. "If we say, 'We have fellowship with him,' while continuing to walk in darkness, we are liars and do not act in truth. But if we walk in light, as he is in the light, we have fellowship with one another" (1 John 1:6-7). In the Christian economy, in other words, evidence of union with God surfaces in some form of love of one another, in "joy, peace, patient endurance, kindness, generosity, faith, mildness, and chastity" (Gal 5:22) not to mention friendship, community, and solidarity.

If we agree that the measure of our union with God is our union with one another, then we must examine more closely the statement that the Eucharist makes both to us who celebrate it and to those who observe us. The chapter by Kenan Osborne alludes to the importance of the Second Vatican Council's naming of the Church as the sacrament of unity.[34] The council also insisted that the Eucharist is the primary way by which the Church's unity is both "signified and brought about."[35] This unity is not to be abstract or mystical but concrete, social, evident, and verifiable. The sign of this unity is not the Eucharist as such but the community brought about by the Eucharist. To be a sign of unity, there has to be a community resulting from it, a community of human beings whose relationship with one another is such that the neutral observer can notice and judge their bondedness. If it is a sign, observers will be able to see something which points beyond the community. If the Church is constructing such signs, the Church is doing what it is to do; it is on course in its mission. If these signs are absent or only ambiguously present, the chances are good that the participants in the Eucharist are not becoming members of one another in any real way.

The Eucharist is a sign in action, the primary part of which is the coming together for the breaking of the bread. The Eucharist's significative power grows to the degree that the participants find Christ to be real food for their hunger. But the bread of life is both consumed and consuming. The Eucharist is a dangerous food to eat, because it makes its consumers become what they eat. They become what they eat if they become bread for one another. The sign action begins with the action of breaking bread and ends with being bread that is broken for others. Being broken, being consumed, losing what they have been given, freely laying down what they are and have for others, they find life. This life is not simply interior or eschatological. They find what the wily manager in Luke's Gospel found he had when he dealt with his master's debtors. He had friends for himself through the use of this world's goods, so that when those goods failed a lasting reception was his (see Luke 16:9).

The consumer culture is meant to have something new to contend with, a new sign to read as a result of Eucharist. The new sign will be a people with a new allegiance, one that goes beyond the care and feeding of the microeconomic unit of the self, the family, the household. This new, wider allegiance to one another will show itself in all the tangible acts of caring and sharing and being cared for and shared with that lead one to realize that one's wealth is the Lord and his friends. It should be obvious that the quality of Christian community is not at this point yet, with some few exceptions here and there. That is why I say we are guilty of understating the Eucharist. Maybe it would be more precise to say that the Eucharist suffers from a lack of expectation about the power it is meant to unleash. It will unleash it if the people who celebrate it become the sign it could make them. If we become the bread we eat, the sign will be there to be read.

Eucharist is too easily reified. By reified I mean made a thing, something separate from those who come together to offer themselves to God in praise and thanksgiving. Disgorged from life and the people who offer themselves, the Eucharist is reifically received, and the offerers resume their chores with the self-understanding that preceded their coming together. Instead of the Eucharist becoming us, it becomes another commodity; Eucharist becomes an it rather than a we. If the Eucharist is not reified, then the self-dispositions of those who come together will be like so many "grains of wheat that were once scattered on the hillsides" but now come together to be transubstantially affected as grains which become bread are.[36] If the Eucharist is not reified, then *we* become other, rather than the host becoming other. Or better, we become other with the host symbolizing the transubstantiation.

The insights the Church has developed over time about "the real presence" must be extended to the people who are the real presence of Christ in their times and places. The condition, after faith, hope, and love that makes a people this real presence, is that they have been changed in their deepest self-sense into bread. They come from isolation to compose one loaf and with one faith, one Lord, and one hope go forth to be grain again by falling onto the ground of the world for the transubstantiation of the whole into the wholeness that the Kingdom of God will be. Although this is figurative language, it should not be allowed to become mystical. Since the Church never becomes more Church than when it comes together for the Eucharist, it is imperative that the concreteness of life in Christ be conveyed at that time and by that means.

Is the Eucharist a means? To some degree this would seem to be the case, but Eucharist also transcends the category. As an event and an action it is its own reason for being done. It is an end in itself. It is thanksgiving and the praise of the community to God the Father through the Son in the Spirit. At the same time the Eucharist functions beyond the event and the action, insofar as the concelebrants become Eucharist for one another and the world to which they return. In this sense Eucharist is a means, since the members of the Body become instrumental in Christ drawing all to himself: "and I—once I am lifted up from earth—will draw all . . . [peoples and things] to myself"[37] (John 12:32).

It should be clear by now why intentional communities are so important to the Eucharist being Eucharist. Eucharist must be a statement about union—with God and with one another. Unless there are communities to prove that a Christian form of union is developing, it is at best a sign with an indistinct or misleading message. Intentional communities make it highly unlikely that the Eucharist will any longer signify a union that is simply between "the soul" and God with no appreciable social realization.

The social evidence which grounds and verifies union with God must be more than the natural bonding of mates, families, blood relatives, ad hoc associations, or affinities born of natural attraction or mutual benefit. I say more than these, because any one of these natural bondings can be the start of something bigger. But the social evidence of union with God must be human unions born from above. The evidence that they are born from above is that these unions reflect the life of Love which is peculiarly God's, as we have seen. But they must also be a human union of human beings. All things being equal, to the degree that the union has composed itself into groups that are intentional, the more credible they will be. By intentional community I mean one that is larger than a family but smaller than geographically determined groups such as most parishes are. Groups that come together because they are chosen into being by the participant members are intentional ecclesial communities, as we understand them in this project. Their characteristics are spelled out in the Westerhoff chapter. They are composed of *Gemeinschaft* relationships, because they encompass human beings in their full personalities rather than *Gesellschaft* relationships, meaning the group touches only one aspect of the person, for example, their need to worship. Hence the members do not relate to one another in any emotional way or with any degree of intimacy.

It would be misleading to suggest that the deficiencies are only in the manner of the celebration of Eucharist and in the self-dispositions of its concelebrants. The problem is also very much in the structures from which the concelebrants come. The American culture, like any culture, is a mixture of unique characteristics that make Americans who they are as a people and destructive tendencies that continually unmake them personally and in the myriad associations that comprise a culture. At the heart of what is good and bad in our culture is our American economy. It has brought our standard of living, materially construed at least, to a higher point than any modern nation has known. It continues to absorb more and more immigrants with relative success and to create more and more jobs for its citizens. It is also an essential part of the international economy's relative health and vitality.

Inimical Forces in American Culture

We all know the other half of the story even better. We know that the good features of the economy have alarmingly dysfunctional effects on the self-understandings, the fortunes, and the social and spiritual life of each one of us. These dysfunctional effects which have seeped into and perverted our culture are interpreted and analysed endlessly. One of the most recent and best analyses, *Habits of the Heart, Individualism and Commitment in American Life*, has researched and established what our intuitions already know, namely, that "we have largely lost the language we need to make moral sense out of our private and public lives."[38] Instead we speak foreign languages to ourselves and to one another. These almost forgotten foreign languages, the authors contend, are the languages of moral discourse, which come from "communities of memory."[39] These must be retrieved, recovered, and reentered. These communities knew and inculcated practises: for example, common worship that enabled citizens to attain to a sense of wonder and common values that enabled them to impede or transcend radical individualism. Absent these languages and their traditions, and we find ourselves brought to a cultural, collective poverty "as absolute as that of the poorest."[40] Eucharistic communities, intentional ones especially, can be compared to a language lab where second languages become the common language of a many who can then become one.

In many ways the issue of the discernment of the dominant culture by the Eucharistic communities, a discernment that affirms its positive features, can be seen as a boundaries issue. A community is a community if it knows itself, stands for things that differentiate it from the dominant culture, and locates itself within certain boundaries: affective, moral, relational, spiritual, doctrinal, theological, liturgical. When the boundaries are unclear, the community is in trouble. The evidence that the boundaries are beginning to blur is when the allegiances of the members are diffused. Their members become attached to things and influences that affect their primary allegiance. The situation becomes even more confused when the individuals learn to deal with plural allegiances by developing a split consciousness and, rather than name this for what it is, take this bifurcated affectivity to be normalcy. By split consciousness I mean the equivalent of the right hand not knowing what the left hand is doing. Hence one can live a fervent religious life in one compartment of heart, mind, and consciousness and live another way entirely in other areas of life. The Second Vatican Council considered the "split between the faith which many profess and their daily lives . . . among the more serious errors of our age."[41] The best example of this split, one which has run through this chapter as a subtheme, is the widely accepted way of life many Americans have learned to live. In part they adhere to "communities of memory" being influenced by their sense of values, and in part they live as adherents of American "economism" with its imperious, ersatz values effectively dictating meaning to them in terms of consumption and material and financial security.

Plural Allegiances

Rather than take on this whole problem, which has been the problem of Western civilization, no less—especially since the Enlightenment—I only want to touch on one aspect of it, namely the issue of allegiances. These seem inevitable. Allegiance implies a preference for, or a loyalty and a commitment to, a particular person or group. These are usually rooted in blood ties, past associations, common interests, or common experiences. The allegiance can be personal, to the persons in question or to a group because of what its members stand for. Christians have to be always concerned to try to integrate their plural allegiances in and around their reportedly deepest allegiance, namely to Christ.

The Pauline insight into Christ and Christianity would not be content to leave the matter there. Paul would contend that one's primary allegiance to Christ included an allegiance to him in his members. A Christian's commitment to Christ would not simply be a commitment to the transcendent Risen Lord but would also be to the historical, empirical, and social component that was intrinsic to his mystery, namely, the community through whom each member received his or her life and with whom each member grew in union with God and towards whom each member committed himself or herself. Paul realized how easily an allegiance to Christ could transcendentalize itself. The nascent gnosticism of Corinthian Christianity was becoming masterful at this form of rationalization, as we have seen. Paul insisted, as we saw, on a bottom line, fleshy understanding of the Christ mystery. Briefly put: every time you eat this bread and drink this cup, realize that you proclaim the death of the Lord (he did not say his resurrection) until he comes in glory (see 1 Cor 11:26). A subsequent epistle clarified this: "I wish to know Christ and the power flowing from his resurrection; likewise to know how to share in his sufferings by being formed into the pattern of his death. Thus do I hope that I may arrive at resurrection from the dead" (Phil 3:10-11). He was very aware that his own passage to resurrection would be mediated by Christ suffering in his members, and before Paul's own resurrection from the dead would take place, this suffering form of the Christ mystery would be a constant way by which he could manifest his allegiance to the Risen Christ, whose power enabled him to share in the suffering of his members.

Christians had to learn how to be very particular about their allegiances to Christ and one another, and at the same time to be all-inclusive. In other words, they had to learn what the Master had learned about particularity and universality. When people in their humanity approached him with their needs, their hopes, or their unfreedoms, he attended to them. He saw the influences that functioned like sovereignties over them and bound them fast. These confused their allegiance to God and one another. These he refused to pay homage to and freed them from. The boundaries observed by Jesus of Nazareth, in other words, were as wide as people and as narrow as the tradition of celebration and interpretation that faithful Israel continued to have in Jesus' day. The sovereignties were not the systems as such, whether they be political, economic, religious, or legal, but the power they had come to be invested with, because people over time had tried to gain something for themselves from them by obeying them sometimes in ruthless spite of their allegiance to God and to other people. Allegiances were the stuff that made reigns. When people placed themselves under reigns that were not under God, the sought for kingdom of God was all the more delayed in its realization.

The comprehensive character of Jesus' allegiances is well summarized in the Lord's Prayer. These allegiances are: the Father, the coming Kingdom of God, the will of God, and people—hence their need for bread and for forgiveness of one another, freedom from bondage and from temptation to make allegiances not ordered by these prior ones. When allegiances are not aligned to and integrated into these primary allegiances, they become objects of obedience and service and trust, thus aping the obedience, trust, and service due to God alone. This is what idolatry is, not idolatry in the sense of worship paid to gods but in the sense of assigning worth, attention, and trust to something less than God or people connected to God. Vagrant allegiances are on their way to creating reigns, sovereignties, and idols. Jesus noted this. "You can't serve God and mammon" (see Matt 6:24). Mammon here is not the economic system of Jesus' day. Its etymology implies that it is the use of financial resources in such a way that they become an alternate object of our trust.[42] If they will care for you, God becomes only one of several gods to whom you can trust your life.

There is a secondary paradigm in 1 Corinthians, which we have looked at briefly, which brings together these several insights about the intentional community's boundaries. It is the matter of eating meat at the temples. Since they confessed Jesus to be their Lord, they were to distance themselves from even an implicit homage to other lords. While they remained in the world, they were not to live there as those who were of it (see 1 Cor 7:29-31). All the things of the world were theirs, but "you are Christ's, and Christ is God's" (1 Cor 3:23). There were no neutral zones, where a Christian was simply outside the context of his or her allegiance to Christ. By imagining that some areas, like the temples, were neutral, they were diluting the Corinthian Christ presence by confusing those who were outside of it, merely observing it, and those who were part of it, trying to live up to its challenge. By projecting a neutrality onto such a structure and its meal custom, which induced or implied an allegiance, Corinthian Christians were creating boundary confusion. "If someone sees you, with your 'knowledge' [that an idol is really nothing], reclining at table in the temple of an idol, may not his conscience in its weak state be influenced to the point that he eats the idol-offering? Because of your 'knowledge' the weak one perishes [because he has acted on an erroneous conscience], that brother for whom Christ died" (1 Cor 8:10-11). Furthermore, "When you sin thus against your brothers and wound their weak consciences, you are sinning against Christ" (1 Cor 8:12).

The coherence of the Body of Christ was being jeopardized by all of those who sought to establish false boundaries. There were those who sought to tighten it and cordon it off from the rest of Corinth and those who sought to intellectualize it with "knowledge" that did not come from or lead to love. There were those who were happy to be members of the new religion but were not prepared to live in a wholly new way and those who sought to liberalize it and enjoy a freedom that refused the discipline of being members of the Body. Paul was anxious to establish the fact that they were not Corinth's nor were they their own. They were Christ's and were brought by him into the field of force that was the Body of Christ or Trinitarian *koinonia*. This meant that one was brought into the powers of communion and self-donation or union and dispossession that are at work within the relationships between Father, Son, and Spirit.

There could hardly be any doubt in those who have hankered for community, sought community, and sought to build community that it does not "work" if it is approached by each seeking to hold on to what they have and at the same time add community for their unmet needs. Community happens where the needs of all are met or at least taken into account. But meeting needs, our own and others', will not come to any depths if we do not share ourselves, our faith, our vulnerability, and to some degree at least our material goods. Our deepest needs may well be immaterial, but any community, if it is to be composed of humans, will show its love of one another in ways that are materially embodied.

Because of who the community is and, therefore, who each of the members are, Paul was concerned that their use of monies and resources testify to their holy communality (see 2 Cor 8 and 9). Yet he was equally concerned not to make their gifts compulsory, since that would indicate that love had not inspired them. Equally loathsome would be the spelling out of a new series of observances redolent of the passé form of achieving righteousness. Their material resources were goods with which God had blessed them. They were to share them with one another with the same love from which they had first come to them. Material resources and monies were part of that which was passing away. They could be retrieved from the world which was passing away if they were used in such wise that their use was determined by love.

In Pauline eschatology the institutions of this world and all the material goods we have or do not have are part and parcel of a form of this-worldliness which is passing away. In the meantime love is to be the principle determining their use. Paul is neither concerned about the future form of the world nor the present form of the world (or its institutions). His concern is that love be the force that operates in the members, and by operating out of that love, the members make use of this world's goods in such a way that they seek not their own interests but those of their neighbors.

Paul's expectations about all of this coming about were fervent, fervid, in fact transcendent, because they were not lodged in the moral life of Christians but on the love (Christ's for them and God's for his Son and them) which gave the Christians life and moral strength. Even before they finished the task which God would do in and through them, they were victorious: "we are more than conquerors because of him who has loved us" (Rom 8:37). Their eschatological relationship to the things of time would give them a dialectical disposition: "buyers should conduct themselves as though they owned nothing, and those who make use of the world as though they were not using it, for the world as we know it is passing away" (1 Cor 7:30-31).

One thing likely to make modern Christians suspicious of this line of reflection and markedly unenthusiastic for what it calls for is that they experience only the self-donation half of it. They know a Christianity that is ever urgent about "give," but they seldom experience a Christian community in which the members are concerned about and care for them. Insofar as this communality and mutuality are wanting, we must insist with ourselves and one another on making use of the double energy that is at work in the trinitarian field of force. To know only the dispossession/self-donation half of it (or only the communion/union half, for that matter) is to miss the peculiar form of social wholeness that being brought into the *koinonia* of God calls for. Therefore they know only half of what God would have us be, diaconal, and not the other half, the communion and consolation of many being made one. These diaconal energies seem to be more expected than the experience of love in Christ.

I am convinced that Christianity is an explosion still to go off, a revolutionary idea still to be comprehended, a banquet in time and history that has been barely nibbled at, and a source of social change the dimensions of which are not even being dreamed of.

These potentialities remain stuck in the still-to-be status because of the way we go about Eucharist—what we bring to it, what we bring from it. For that reason I think Christianity's potentiality will move to actuality only if the Eucharist is celebrated in a different way and with a different perspective than it ordinarily is today. This chapter has tried to show that we do not need to devise alternative forms of worship, but that we need to worship according to the alternative we have become in Christ.

Footnotes

1. Pope John Paul II, *On Human Work* (Washington: United States Catholic Conference, 1982) 44.

2. American Bishops, "Catholic Social Teaching and the U.S. Economy," first draft, *Origins* 14, no. 22/23, 350.

3. *The Documents of Vatican II*, ed. Walter Abbott, "Pastoral Constitution on the Church in the Modern World" 264.

4. Joseph Slinger, "Sociological Theory," unpublished manuscript.

5. Jerome Murphy-O'Connor, *Becoming Human Together* (Wilmington: Michael Glazier 1982). Excellent introduction to Pauline anthropology in Corinthian letters.

6. Gunther Bornkamm, *Early Christian Experience* (London: SCM Press, 1969) 149.

7. William F. Orr and James Walther, *1 Corinthians: A New Translation*, The Anchor Bible (Garden City, N.Y.: Doubleday, 1976) 270.

8. C.F.D. Moule, "The Judgment Theme in the Sacraments," *The Background of the New Testament and Its Eschatology*, eds. W.D. Davies and D. Daube (Cambridge University Press, 1956) 467-9.

9. E. Kasemann, "The Pauline Doctrine of the Last Supper," *Essays on New Testament Themes* (Naperville, Ill: A.R. Allenson, 1964) 120.

10. O'Connor, *Becoming Human Together* 92-94.

11. Bornkamm, *Early Christian Experience* 151-2.

12. Jerome Murphy-O'Connor, *St. Paul's Corinth* (Wilmington: Michael Glazier, 1983). This volume cites all the ancient sources which defame Corinth, and also cites evidence to the contrary.

13. C. K. Barrett, *The First Epistle to the Corinthians* (New York: Harper and Row, 1968) 5.

14. Jerome Murphy-O'Connor, "Eucharist and Community in First Corinthians" *Worship*, 50 (1976) 375.

15. *Ibid.*

16. Joseph A. Fitzmyer, *Pauline Theology* (Englewood Cliffs, N.J.: Prentice-Hall, 1967) 61. Also Barrett, *The First Epistle* 149.

17. For a New Testament way of saying this, see Luke 1:35.

18. X. Leon-Dufour, *Resurrection and the Message of Easter* (New York: Holt, Rinehart and Winston, 1975) 271.

19. Friedrich Have, "Koinos," *Theological Dictionary of the New Testament*, ed. Gerhard Kittell (Grand Rapids: Eerdmans, 1964) 3-798.

20. *Ibid.* 795.

21. *Ibid.* 796.

22. Bornkamm, *Early Christian Experience* 189.

23. *Ibid.*

24. Hans Conzelmann, *A Commentary on the First Epistle to the Corinthians* (Philadelphia: Fortress Press, 1975) 172.

25. *Ibid.* 15.

26. *Ibid.* 173.

27. *Ibid.* 193.

28. Barrett, *The First Epistle* 48.

29. *Ibid.* 50.

30. *Ibid.* 53.

31. Karl Rahner, "An Investigation of the Incomprehensibility of God in Thomas Aquinas," *Theological Investigations* (New York: Seabury, 1979) 16 = 244-254.

32. Orr and Walther, *I Corinthians*, 250.

33. Conzelmann, *Commentary on Corinthians* 172.

34. *Documents of Vatican II* 147.

35. *Ibid.* 343.

36. This prayer is taken from "The Didache," chapter 9. *The Didache (and other Epistles)*, ed. James Kleist (London: Longmans, Green and Co. 1961) 20.

37. Raymond Brown, *The Gospel According to John (I-XII)* The Anchor Bible (Garden City, N.Y.: Doubleday, 1968) 468. He cites an alternate reading, a neuter plural, which suggests more than people being drawn to Christ.

38. Robert N. Bellah and others, *Habits of the Heart; Individualism and Commitment in American Life* (Berkeley: University of California Press, 1985) 292.

39. *Ibid.* 152-153.

40. *Ibid.* 296.

41. *Documents of Vatican II* 243.

42. Joseph A. Fitzmyer, "The Story of the Dishonest Manager, Lk 16: 1-13," *Essays on the Semitic Background of the New Testament* (London: Geoffrey, Chapman, 1971) 170.

Bibliography

I. *The Linkage:*

Searle, Mark, ed. *Liturgy and Social Justice.* Collegeville: The Liturgical Press, 1980. Four essays that attempt to connect the two concerns related to this chapter.

Haughey, John C., ed. *The Faith that Does Justice,* New York: Paulist Press, 1977. A series of essays on the interaction of faith and justice. Most pertinent to this chapter is D. Hollenbach's "A Prophetic Church and the Catholic Sacramental Imagination."

Schmidt and Power, eds. *Politics and Liturgy,* Concilium, new series, vol. 2, no. 2. Several articles in this collection are worth noting, for example, Gelineau's "Celebrating the Paschal Liberation" and David Power's "The Song of the Lord in an Alien Land."

Balasuriya, Tissa, *The Eucharist and Human Liberation*. Maryknoll, N.Y.: Orbis Books, 1979. Hellwig, Monika, *The Eucharist and the Hunger of the World* (New York: Paulist Press, 1976). Two forays into the social impact the sacrament is meant to have on the distribution of the world's goods.

II. *Commentaries on the First Letter to the Corinthians:*

Orr, William F., and Walther, James. *1 Corinthians: A New Translation*, The Anchor Bible. Garden City, N.Y.: Doubleday, 1976.

Barrett. C.K. *The First Epistle to the Corinthians*. New York: Harper & Row, 1968.

Conzelmann, Hans. *A Commentary on the First Epistle to the Corinthians*. Philadelphia: Fortress Press, 1975.

III. *Useful Books:*

Murphy-O'Connor, Jerome. *St. Paul's Corinth*. Wilmington: Michael Glazier, 1983.

Murphy-O'Connor, Jerome. *Becoming Human Together*. Wilmington: Michael Glazier, 1982.

Bellah, Robert N. and others. *Habits of the Heart; Individualism and Commitment in American Life* Berkeley: University of California Press, 1985.

Robinson, John A.T. *The Body*. Philadelphia: Westminster, 1959.

IV. *Useful Articles:*

Kasemann, E. "The Pauline Doctrine of the Last Supper," *Essays on New Testament Themes*, Studies in Biblical Theology #41. Naperville, Ill: A. R. Allenson, 1964.

Kasemann, E. "On Paul's Anthropology" and "The Theological Problem Presented by the Motif of the Body of Christ," *Perspectives on Paul*. Philadelphia: Fortress Press, 1971.

Moiser, John. "A Promise of Plenty: The Eucharist as Social Critique," *Downside Review* 91, #305 (Oct. 1973).

Egan, John J. "Liturgy and Social Action," *Origins*, 13, pp. 245 ff.

Bornkamm, Gunther. "Lord's Supper and Church in Paul"; "On the Understanding of Worship"; "The More Excellent Way;" *Early Christian Experience* London: SCM Press, 1969.

Barrett C. K. "Things Sacrificed to Idols," *Essays on Paul*. Philadelphia: Westminster, 1982.

Haughey, John C. "Eucharist at Corinth: You are the Christ," *Above Every Name*, ed. Thomas E. Clarke. New York: Paulist Press, 1980.

3. EUCHARISTIC THEOLOGY TODAY

Kenan Osborne, O.F.M.

Introduction

Within the last one hundred years (1880-1980) there has been
a great deal of theological effort as regards the Christian sacraments,
both by Roman Catholic and by Protestant authors. Indeed some
of this effort can be characterized as radical, revolutionary, and
nontraditional. This kind of theological thinking has caused concern both in Catholic and in Protestant circles. Assuredly it would
be far beyond the scope of this present chapter to develop all the
reasons for this theological climate, but the following pages take
up issues which have special merit in any discussion on the contemporary theology of the sacraments and in particular on the sacrament of the Eucharist. These ideas will help to indicate the reasons
for this "radicalness" in contemporary sacramental and Eucharistic theology.

The focus of this entire book is on the social nature of the Eucharist and the role which social sciences bear on the matter. John
Westerhoff, for instance, in the section on the Eucharist within
America, describes the variety of influences which permeate North
American culture. Such cultural influences do appear in Eucharistic celebrations by North Americans, and yet the roots for the present
change in Eucharistic theology are not North American but for the
most part European. Even liturgically North Americans borrowed
heavily from the Europeans, at least at first. St. John's Abbey in
Collegeville, Minnesota, between the two world wars was a major

center of liturgical thought, but the dependence on Europe was clear. The genius of the North American scholar, particularly during and after the Second Vatican Council, has been to take some of this European material and reshape it along social lines. Indeed the social sciences have been thriving in the United States, and it has been primarily through very recent efforts of North American theologians that the findings of the social sciences have begun to appear in any substantive way in theological discussion. It seems necessary, therefore, to locate the bases, even though they are predominantly European, for the Eucharistic theology which our scholars and liturgists in the United States are today expressing both theoretically and practically.

The Second Vatican Council can be seen as a watershed for contemporary sacramental theology, since many of the changes were endorsed and furthered by the council. Still it would be a complete misreading of the council documents if one were to see in them the causes for this sacramental development. Long before the council theologians were already at work; changes had already been established; implications had begun to be drawn. In a positive but cautious way, the Second Vatican Council allied itself with this contemporary approach to sacramental theology. However, since the council documents in no way focused exclusively on the sacraments in general or on the Eucharist in a specific way, the thought of the Second Vatican Council can be ascertained only in a general and sometimes tangential way.

Nonetheless, five factors seem to merit special consideration on this matter of change or development in contemporary Eucharistic theology.

First, there has been the rise of historical consciousness and therefore of historical scholarship regarding the Christian sacraments. This has occurred theologically especially during the past one hundred years. Perhaps more than any other factor this historical research in sacramental history has played a dominant role in the reconsideration of the traditional approach to the sacraments. More than any other council in the history of the Church, the Second Vatican Council was attuned to and respectful of historical data. We will return to this matter further on in this chapter.

Second, there has been the renewal of biblical interpretation. Although Roman Catholic scholars were at first cautioned on this matter by official Church statements, due to the Modernist threat of the late nineteenth and early twentieth centuries, these biblical scholars soon moved beyond the Modernist positions, which were causing the problems, and into the mainstream of the contemporary biblical renewal. This is particularly evident from 1940 onward, although there were indeed Roman Catholic biblical scholars prior to 1940 who did tremendous groundwork in the biblical renewal. Nonetheless, the publication of the encyclical *Divino Afflante Spiritu* by Pope Pius XII in 1943 provided one of the strongest incentives for the Catholic renewal of biblical scholarship.[1] Quite naturally the renewal of biblical interpretation provided the traditional approach to sacramental theology with new biblical tools and new hermeneutical methods. Since the Eucharist plays a dominant role in the New Testament, the reinterpretation of the biblical data on the Eucharist gave rise to many new insights into Eucharistic theology generally. Of particular importance in this matter was the study of ancient biblical languages, such as Hebrew, Aramaic, and Greek, as well as other cognate languages used by the early Church, such as Syriac, Coptic, and Phoenician. At the end of the nineteenth century and in the first part of the twentieth century, The Catholic University of America in Washington, D.C., was one of the outstanding centers for the teaching of such languages. Many American biblical scholars were thus well trained for the historical study of the Bible, which was a major part of the renewal of biblical interpretation.

Third, the philosophical approach of contemporary Anglo-American and European thinkers has challenged the somewhat entrenched position of Scholastic theology, that is, the philosophical basis of such theologians as St. Thomas Aquinas. More pointedly the attempt by Pope Leo XIII and other Catholic European scholars to emphasize neo-Scholasticism met with only a brief success. Indeed the influence of European philosophies like existentialism, and the philosophical method of phenomenology on Roman Catholic theology has been widespread and has affected theological development both directly and indirectly. Existentialism is that style of philosophy begun in the main by such thinkers as Sören Kierkegaard and Friedrich Nietzsche. Their emphasis was not on the abstract but on the concrete, not on essence but on existence. Essence or substance for them is abstract and unhistorical. Somewhat later the phenomenological method began to develop. Its main proponents were Edmund Husserl and his successor, Martin Heidegger. It is basically a method which proceeds from the analysis of human experience rather than from universal and metaphysical categories.[2]

Indeed the entire discussion on transignification, as contrasted with transubstantiation, can be understood only on the basis of an appreciation of contemporary phenomenology. Beyond this strong and profound influence of existentialism and phenomenology on Roman Catholic theology, the North American scholar has moved cautiously and somewhat slowly into the area of a third contemporary philosophical movement, namely, that of process modes of thought. Process modes of thought were systematically asserted by an English scholar, Alfred North Whitehead, who had made a career in mathematics and physics. This mathematical and physical science base is particularly close to the North American understanding of life, and it is primarily North American scholars who developed this line of thought, and it is primarily North American Roman Catholic theologians who began to utilize such process modes of thought in their own theological endeavors. In many ways this approach is uniquely North American. At this present writing one can say that process thought has developed rather strongly as a philosophy, but it has moved more slowly as a theology, even here in the United States.

Fourth, and largely through the influence of liberation theology from Latin America, the emphasis on the social dimension of the sacraments cannot be overlooked. Even though liberation theology has been challenged recently by Pope John Paul II and other Vatican offices, still it would be quite unscholarly not to see that there has been a clear relationship between liberation theology on the one hand and the social theological emphasis of contemporary sacramental theology on the other, with a special emphasis on contemporary Eucharistic theology. Indeed the efforts of liberation theologians have brought sharp focus to the social implications of Christian life generally and to baptismal and Eucharistic theology in particular. The tendency to make the sacraments more or less private matters of faith and conscience dominated the traditional approach to sacramental Roman Catholic theology in the nineteenth century and the early part of the twentieth century. This private and individual approach has been radically set aside by liberation theologians. It is, of course, quite evident that the liberation theology of Latin America cannot simply be transplanted to the North American or the European scene without a process of reinterpretation and inculturation. Still liberation theology cannot be discounted by scholars today, since it has seriously influenced sacramental theology. Sociological frameworks and implications are still being studied by current authors on sacramental theology. This socio-logical framework has highlighted in a profound way the incultu-ration process both in the sacramental life of the Church (praxis) and in the theologizing on such sacramental life (theory).

Fifth, and finally, the ecumenical stance of the Roman Catholic Church requires the contemporary rethinking of sacramental the-ology from the standpoint of Protestant-Catholic relationships. This entails both a positive and at times negative evaluation of the sacramental life and theology of the other Christian Churches, and in light of this evaluation a critical reexamination of the sacramen-tal life and theology of the Roman Catholic approach. Since ecumenism clearly and officially does not mean a "return to Mother Church," the corresponding study of the sacramental positions of the Protestant Christian Churches cannot mean that these non-Roman Catholic positions are valid only in that they correspond to the prevailing Roman Catholic stance. Rather, ecumenism is the realization that "Church" is clearly found in the strands of the Chris-tian community—Protestant, Orthodox, and Roman Catholic— and since one cannot truly have "Church" without sacraments, then the sacramental positions of the various Christian communities need to be reconsidered more positively than ever before. In the United States, where Protestants and Roman Catholics live in such an in-terconnected way, this ecumenical influence is of serious social proportions.

Against this grid of influence, let us now turn to each of them in a more detailed way. Once again, however, we must remember that these five areas are only five of the major areas which have affected the renewal of theological thinking in post-Second Vati-can Council theology. In the United States the Roman Catholic Church has from colonial times been very open socially, but quite traditional theologically. Most of the American bishops in the last two centuries have reflected this dual stance: social issues have been championed by the Roman Catholic Church in the United States, but new approaches to theology have generally been repressed. The North American Church, theologically, has been dominated by Eu-ropean ways of thinking and European ways of liturgy. Some ef-forts were of course made in opposition to this European approach, but these efforts really did not begin to flourish until the era of the Second Vatican Council. The social sciences were not and are not alien to the Church in the United States, but until quite recently the North American Church was not at all ready to allow the social sciences to influence theological and liturgical life. Actually it took a change in Europe (through the five points just enumerated, which are not North American in origin) to bring about a rethinking of our sacramental and Eucharistic theology. Still one perceives in North American Church life a real polarity at times and a struggle against such new ways of thinking one's faith. This is due in no small measure to our Church history in the United States.

An Historicized Understanding of the Eucharist

As far as Roman Catholic theology is concerned, it is perhaps the publication of H.C. Lea's book *A History of Auricular Confession and Indulgences in the Latin Church*,[3] a publication which appeared in three volumes in 1896, that moved Roman Catholic scholarship into an intense study of historical development not only of the sacrament of penance but of all the sacraments. Since Lea's book was so obviously anti-Catholic, a Catholic response was clearly needed. At that time the only Catholic scholars who had any expertise on the matter were patrologists, that is, scholars who studied the early Fathers of the Church, such as F. X. Funk, P. Battifol, E. Vacandard, and P. A. Kirsch. These scholars, although combatting the anti-Catholic stance of Lea, found many areas in which they agreed with him. Such an openness, however, was not accepted by the major dogmatic theologians of that time, like Gartmeier, Di Dario, and Pignataro. These Catholic dogma professors reacted negatively to the Catholic patrologists, since many of the historical findings did not coincide with the then acceptable dogmatic stance which they were teaching. Shortly afterward, however, a new generation of Catholic scholars turned to the historical data and pursued the matter more thoughtfully. These Catholic authors included such notable personages as Huenermann, D'Ales, Tixeront, Rauschen, Galtier, Poschmann, and K. Rahner.

In the early Church penance was closely allied to baptism; indeed it was called the "second plank" after baptism for those Christians who found themselves shipwrecked by serious sin. As a result the history of penance involved a history of baptism as well, and we are today extremely privileged as scholars to have solid studies on the history both of baptism and of penance. One can detect, however, a chain reaction in sacramental theology, since both baptism and penance had close ties with the Eucharist, baptism as the "door" to the Eucharist and penance as the reopening of the "door" to the Eucharist after Eucharistic excommunication. As a result the history of the Mass and Eucharistic devotion began to be studied. Today we have many excellent histories of the Eucharist, even though all the historical questions have not yet been resolved. Since the Eucharist cannot be understood without its connection to the sacrament of orders, and since most of the scholars involved were clerics themselves, historical studies on the priesthood began to fare rather well, while historical research on confirmation, anointing of the sick, and marriage trailed noticeably.

In general one could say that there was some unevenness in these works on the historical development of the sacraments. This is due to the tendency, here and there, to maintain an apologetic approach to the dogmatic and traditional teaching on the sacraments. It was not a question of opposing or defending any of the defined teachings on the sacraments by the Roman Catholic Church; rather, it was a maintaining of the somewhat narrow Scholastic approach to sacramental theology. Indeed Scholastic sacramental theology, whether from the eleventh and twelfth centuries or from the Counter-Reformation of the sixteenth and seventeenth centuries, was restricted and narrow, since the rich historical data, available to scholarship today, was generally unavailable to these Scholastic authors. As a result the Scholastic authors theologized on the sacramental practice of their day, proposing this kind of theological framework as what had "always been in the Church." The method was dogmatic and unhistorical, while today the method is much more historical and heuristic.

The integration of such historical material into the dogmatic approach to Roman Catholic theology has been a slow process. A. Tanquerey's *Brevior Synopsis Theologiae Dogmaticae*, which was a standard text for most Catholic seminaries, was translated and published by J. J. Byrnes as late as 1959. Although there is some slight utilization of historical thought by Tanquerey, he does not move in any significant way beyond the traditional framework of sacramental theology. He uses historical data in a quite apologetic way. What is of note is that such a book would be translated and published on the eve of the Second Vatican Council and still have a great deal of popularity.

Another indication of this slow integration of historical data into the theologizing of the Catholic Church is offered by a sacramental historian himself, B. Neunheuser. In his volume *Eucharistie in Mittelalter und Neuzeit* (Eucharist in the Middle Ages and the Modern Period),[4] the author takes us from the middle of the seventh century through the period of the Council of Trent in a lengthy and detailed way. This part of the work is a rather comprehensive presentation of the Latin Scholastic approach to the Eucharist, and for that period it is a scholarly historical study. From the Council of Trent to the present time, the material is summarized in a matter of four pages; this is indicative of the fact that the author really saw nothing new in Roman Catholic thought during those later centuries. Instead, the various Catholic authors of the sixteenth to the twentieth centuries reiterated the traditional, Scholastic approach to the Eucharist, which, as mentioned, was quite unhistorical.

A similar historical approach, but for even an earlier period, is taken by J. Betz in his article "Eucharistie als Zentrales Mysterium" (Eucharist as a Central Mystery) in the series *Mysterium Salutis*.[5] Betz, of course, had previously written at great length on the Eucharist in the Greek world in his book *Die Eucharistie in der Zeit der griechischen Väter* (The Eucharist in the Age of the Greek Fathers).[6] These contributions of Betz indicate the profound, non-Scholastic approach to Eucharistic theology which the early Greek Church has bequeathed to the universal Church.

The history of the Latin Mass has been historically investigated in the monumental works of Jungmann, Fortescue, and Martimort. Jeremias' foundational study *The Eucharistic Words of Jesus*[7] remains a pivotal and historically important New Testament approach to the Eucharist.

The conclusion, which one might draw from this fairly recent scholarly spate of material on the development of the sacraments and on the Eucharist in particular, is this: theologizing was not, in the early centuries of the Church, Scholastic in its approach, and one might add that Scholasticism is simply one way of approaching the theology of the sacraments and of Eucharist. Indeed there has clearly been a history to the very theologizing, and this process of history is not at all completed.

The Biblical Renewal of Eucharistic Interpretation

The New Testament studies of our own century on the Eucharist have been numerous, and the work on this matter is still going on. The Last Supper plays a major role in this interpretative renewal, and the question whether the Last Supper was a Passover meal or not is still not settled. There are solid scholarly reasons for opting one way or the other, and given the limited data which we have, the question might never be resolved. If the Last Supper was not a Passover meal, then its interpretation as such, even within the New Testament itself, is already theologizing. However, since the Passover motif is not uniform in the Eucharistic interpretation of the New Testament, it represents only one way of considering the Eucharist, and not at all the only way. In other words an overly dogmatic approach, based on the Passover interpretation of the Last Supper, needs today to be carefully qualified and nuanced and even open to the possibility that the Last Supper was not a Passover meal at all.

As the New Testament moves into its later stages and provides us with a glimpse of the apostolic and subapostolic Church, we are presented not so much with the fixed interpretations of Scholastic theology but with somewhat hesitant and even soft data on the early Church's celebration of the Eucharist. The Eucharist was at that time situated within a meal complex, and a Jewish meal complex at that, rather than a Graeco-Roman one. At a Jewish meal the host figure was the main male figure of the perhaps wider Jewish family. This point alone raises the question of who might have presided at the early Eucharists. It is historically not at all clear today that in that earliest of Christian periods only an ordained person presided at the Eucharist. That ordination was requisite for such presiding cannot be ascertained by the historical material available to us from the New Testament data nor from the data deriving from the apostolic and subapostolic age. Hervé-Marie Legrand, in his essay "The Presidency of the Eucharist According to the Ancient Tradition," carefully amasses the pertinent material and notes that "in the pre-Nicene period we find cases of presidency more diversified than ours (they cannot be reduced without exception to presidency based on presbyteral-episcopal ordination); but the rule is constant that it pertains to those who preside over the upbuilding of the Church to preside over the sacrament of her unity, over the sacrament which causes her to exist more profoundly in act."[8]

Anyone who is conversant with the current material on the subject realizes the complexity of the issue of ministry in the New Testament and that the precise tasks of the "episkopos" or the "presbyter" are unclear and cannot be measured by the tasks of "bishop" and "priest" today. There has been a clear development of episcopal office and presbyteral office in the Church. Presidency of the Eucharist is not clearly the prerogative of the "episkopos" or the "presbyter" in the New Testament material.

We read in 1 Cor 11:24-25 that Jesus added to the words of institution or words of interpretation the phrase: "Do this in remembrance of me." Many traditional Roman Catholic theologians have interpreted this phrase as an "ordination" phrase. This same kind of interpretation has occurred in official Church documents, not, of course, as though such documents define this interpretation, but rather these documents simply employ a common theological opinion of their times. Still, given the New Testament scholarship of the present age, it would be very difficult to maintain such an opinion. Again, the New Testament is not concerned with ordination in this text, much less with presiding at the Eucharist.

It is also clear from the New Testament and from the documents of the early Church that the Eucharist was celebrated in the context of a meal, with the blessing of the bread at the inception of the meal and the blessing of the cup of wine at the conclusion of the meal. During the meal the people ate, conversed, shared food and life together, much as people today. This connection with the meal lasted into the early Middle Ages, with the Eucharist celebrated with a meal in church on special occasions.

Whatever ritualistic features these meals had, they were based at first on Jewish meal customs, for example, seder, haburah, sabbath. As the number of Christians increased, on the one hand, and the presence of the nonbaptized at such meals began to take place, on the other hand, the Christians felt a pastoral and even theological need to separate the Eucharistic portion of the meal from the repast itself. As a result we have the appearance of non-Eucharistic agapes and also the appearance of a separate Eucharist. This separate Eucharist, that is, separate from a meal, quite naturally began to be liturgized, and models from Jewish synagogue liturgy began to be evident in the Christian celebrations of Eucharist. Much of this liturgizing is not in the New Testament, but is found in the writings of the early Church. The liturgizing developed, therefore, more through pastoral needs than through any divinely preordained formula. Only this pastoral development accounts for the divergent liturgies and liturgical trends which one finds in Church history. Today, therefore, we cannot too readily claim New Testament validation for many of the liturgical aspects of the current celebration of the Eucharist.

One notes that current Eucharistic theology is much more cautious in handling the New Testament Eucharistic material, and is far more open to the dynamics of pastoral development in much of the Eucharistic practice down through the centuries. This helps us today to appreciate tradition and more pointedly traditions in Eucharistic celebrations. There has grown up not only a different liturgical style in the Eastern Churches, but there has also grown up a theologizing of that style which is in no way Scholastic in its approach. In the West there were also several differing liturgical styles, and these too had a theologizing behind them. In the course of history, however, the Gallic-Roman tradition minimized or excluded these other liturgical formulae for celebrating the Eucharist. This multiplicity of Eucharistic celebrations and Eucharistic theologies can be intelligible and acceptable only if the New Testament itself is open to such divergence. Today scholars would say yes to this New Testament openness or nonspecification of definite theological and celebrational detail.

Clearly the real presence of Jesus in the Eucharist is a constant, not only in the New Testament but also in the history of the Church. Remarkably there were no Eucharistic heresies of any note until the ninth century. This alone indicates a widespread unity on the issue of the real presence. It was the specification theologically of this presence in the ninth century and thereafter that caused theological disputes to begin to take place. One can only say that the Western or Latin approach called transubstantiation is but one way in which the presence of Jesus in the Eucharist can be expressed theologically.

Contemporary Philosophical Approaches

It would be difficult today to discuss the New Testament hermeneutical approach without discussing the contributions of Rudolf Bultmann. Still any discussion of Bultmann implies some discussion of existentialism, since existentialism is so much a part of his entire New Testament endeavor. It is interesting to note the influence Bultmann has had, not only on Protestant biblical scholars but also on Roman Catholic biblical authors. If for no other reason than this, the study of existentialism is mandatory for today's theologian.

On the other hand, it has been acknowledged without any hesitation that Karl Rahner has had a lasting influence on the Second Vatican Council and the theology which both preceded and has developed after it. Still one cannot read Rahner without some understanding of Martin Heidegger and the phenomenological approach to contemporary philosophy. Indeed one might say that there is no Roman Catholic theologian alive today who has not been influenced to some degree by Karl Rahner and therefore by phenomenology.

When we turn to the theology of the Eucharist in today's Roman Catholic world, we also see that both existentialism and phenomenology have exerted powerful influences. In the liturgical proclamation of the Word, one can see how important the existential emphasis on the present moment of existence is. It is not a question of simply the Word but of proclaiming the Word. This Word correspondingly must be heard. The exact passage from Scripture can be repeated again and again, but the Word is always heard in the now. One must accept or reject the Word of God coming to him or her at this particular time of life.

Liturgy in itself is totally existential, since each liturgy is celebrated at a new time of life, when each of the members of the community is at a new instance of existence. There is no way of repeating a previous liturgy; liturgy only speaks in the *now*. This is both the beauty and the problem of liturgical action, for it is indeed action which encompasses the moment of a community's life. Rote liturgy in no way speaks to the people; nor does startlingly new liturgy fulfill its promise, since rote liturgy is but a rehash of the past, and startlingly new liturgy does not provide one's moment of present existence with a texture of historical validation. One is so old that the Word is itself made humdrum; the other is so new that the Word is unintelligible, much as new language is unintelligible since there is no texture against which to savor it.

Of far more influence on liturgy, perhaps, is the issue of phenomenology. One cannot begin to understand what current Roman Catholic theologians are saying about transignification unless one has some grasp of phenomenology. The second part of chapter two of Schillebeeckx's book *The Eucharist*[9] is entitled "The New Point of Departure for the Interpretation of the Eucharistic Presence." This new point of departure is the phenomenological approach to reality. The difficulty with Schillebeeckx's position and the position of other similar Catholic theologians who present the transignification theory is not with an understanding of the Council of Trent. Assuredly Schillebeeckx devotes the first part of his book to a reexamination of the teaching of the Council of Trent. Some, such as Gutwenger, have taken issue with Schillebeeckx on this particular matter. Still, whether Schillebeeckx or Gutwenger is correct in their differing views on the conciliar teaching is not at all central to Schillebeeckx's main thrust, the phenomenological view of reality.

At the turn of the century, there were many Roman Catholic theologians who maintained that the connection between an acceptable belief in the real Eucharistic presence of Jesus and the teaching on transubstantiation was intrinsic. That is, one could not deny transubstantiation without at the same time denying the real presence of Jesus in the Eucharist, and conversely, if one believed in the real presence of Jesus in the Eucharist, one had to hold as well the theological position of transubstantiation. J. Piccirelli, a professor at the Gregorianum, maintained this view in his book *The Catholic Understanding of the Dogma of Transubstantiation*, which appeared in 1912. Those who disagreed with his view were called *moderni*, indicating the innovativeness of the stance which maintained that the connection was only extrinsic, that is, one could believe in the real Eucharistic presence of Jesus and not hold the theory of transubstantiation.

It is no wonder, then, that the advocates of transignification met with a hostile audience in some areas of the Roman Church. There were still those who saw the connection as intrinsic, and Schillebeeckx was quite right in saying that a totally new starting point was necessary. This starting point does not derive from a philosophy which is *perennis* nor from a theology which is argued *sub specie aeternitatis*. Rather, the issue is one of human perspective, or as Maurice Merleau-Ponty would say, "the primacy of perception." The way in which human beings at particular points of time and space perceive the world is of utmost importance. Likewise humans perceive the world quite differently than animals, and thus perspective plays a major role. To cite Merleau-Ponty once more, the way you see red and the way I see red may not be the same. We are all individuals, and in our perspectives as individuals, there is a large area of divergence.

Eating is no different. The way animals eat and the way humans eat are quite distinct. A meal is not simply the ingestion of food; rather, the food is indeed part of a meal, but so is the social context and the interpersonal sharing which accompanies a meal. Indeed it is not simply bread and wine, inanimate objects, which are the sacrament of the Eucharist—or as the traditional theologian would say, the *sacramentum tantum*—it is rather the meal which is the sacrament, and this meal included the complexity and the dynamics of people eating together in the context of faith in Jesus.

There is surely no room in this chapter to enter into a discussion on the meaning of phenomenology. This can be found at length elsewhere. It is sufficient here simply to indicate that a preliminary study of the meaning and the implications of the phenomenological method in contemporary philosophy is a sine qua non to any appreciation and understanding of contemporary Eucharistic theology. Nor is there room here to discuss the meaning of existentialism, but whether one is open to the new Eucharistic approaches or is negatively critical of them, no serious consideration or critique can be provided unless a solid acquaintance with both existential thought and the phenomenological method is involved.

The issue of process modes of thought is at present somewhat incipient in theological investigations, but it should be noted that process philosophy will most likely be a strong force within contemporary Catholic theology within the next two decades, and accordingly acquaintance of process modes of thought is likewise imperative for the contemporary serious Catholic scholar on the sacraments and on the Eucharist.

The Influence of Liberation Theology on the Eucharist

One of the more interesting chapters in Juan Segundo's book *The Sacraments Today*[10] is the opening chapter entitled "A New Crisis for the Sacraments?" Segundo states what most people involved in the pastoral activity of the Church already know, namely, that there is a crisis in today's sacramental practice. The fact of the crisis is not what is intriguing in Segundo's position; rather, it is the communitarian or social aspect of the sacraments, which Segundo stresses, that merits center stage. Segundo writes:

> Perhaps the clearest case of all this is the Eucharist—the communitarian sacrament *par excellence*. In the celebration with which we are familiar, the Eucharist brings people next to each other; it juxtaposes them. It does not make a community out of the participants.[11]

Segundo and other major voices from Latin America, are attempting to make the Christian community of their area aware of the social implications in Christianity. There is particular emphasis in their writings on the community aspects of baptism and the Eucharist.

The sacraments within the context of Christian life are some of the major sources which nourish the Christian life. As such we are quite correct to ask whether the sacraments really do assist Christians who share in the sacraments with a deeper social awareness of the Gospel. Do Christians after celebrating the Eucharist leave the altar of the sacrament and go out to the altar of the world and perceive injustice and oppression in any different way than before they celebrated the Eucharist? Does the Eucharist make any difference from a communitarian and social standpoint? Many Christians, priests and pastors included, feel that the parish is thriving if the sacraments, particularly reconciliation and the Eucharist, are well attended. Statistics need to be turned in to diocesan headquarters at regular intervals. No questions about the Christian response to poverty, oppression, violence and injustice are posed, much less whether the sacraments themselves have helped Christians to perceive these injustices within their own neighborhoods. Going to Mass, or going to communion, or going to confession are still very much personal and private matters.

Perhaps the highlight of Segundo's book is found in the chapter "Sacraments That Speak." Since sacraments are indeed signs, they must "say" something. But what do they say, and what is heard? The very efficacy of the sacraments is in their "signing" of grace, not just to an individual but to the Christian community, and from the community to the world surrounding that Christian community. It is this "speaking power" of the sacraments which has been muted, and at times even lost. Sacraments have become rote, and as such what they say and what one hears is a timeless message, as it is called, but precisely as timeless it loses its impact on concrete space and time. Even the liturgizing of the Eucharist is not meant to "speak" to our precise space and time, but only to utter some generalized and timeless words. It is no wonder that Christians leave the Eucharist and have little sensitivity to the social problems of the day. The Gospel's timely message was enveloped by a timeless vacuum. It is only through the regaining of the social dimension of the sacraments that the crisis in today's sacramental practice will begin to abate.

To do this, however, it is necessary to find some new, socially oriented theology of the sacraments. The older theology is privatized and individuated. It goes hand in hand with a spirituality based on the salvation of the individual soul. What is needed is a communitarian theology of the sacraments and one that goes with a spirituality which is other-centered *not* "my-own-soul" centered. This corresponds with the Word of love which crisscrosses every page of the Gospels.

The theology of liberation is a radical stance, not because it derives from some Marxist principles, but rather because it breaks radically with the individualized theology and spirituality of the sacraments, particularly the Eucharist. Traditional Roman Catholic theologians do not feel at home in the area of liberation theology, not because of extraneous factors but because the rootage of the traditional theology of the sacraments has been more strongly placed in a communitarian base. This is not "home territory" for the traditional theologian. But it is the contention of the liberation theologians that it is the "home territory" for the Christian sacraments, since this is precisely the Gospel orientation of the entire Christian life.

It would probably be helpful if the liberation theologians grounded the sacramental theology of the individual sacraments more strongly in the foundation of the Church as a sacrament. Only if the social nature of the Church is made more evident, and this in conjunction with the Second Vatican Council's endorsement of the Church as a foundational sacrament, will the social dimension of the individual sacraments be more visible. The liberation theologians have indeed spent much time on the theology of the Church but not specifically on the idea that the Church is basic sacrament. We still must turn to the European theologians for any detailed study on this matter. But if the social dimension of the individual sacraments is to be made more acceptable, then the social dimension of the Church precisely *qua* sacrament must be made more intrinsic to their position. This is not simply a study of the social dimension of the Church, which the liberation theologians have already done quite well, but it is the study of the social dimension of the Church precisely in its nature as a fundamental sacrament which needs further attention.

The same can be applied to Christology. The current sacramental theology speaks of Jesus in his humanity as *the* basic sacrament. The Christologies of liberation theologians do indeed address the issues of the social impact of Jesus' message and person. What is needed, however, is a focus on the social dimension of Jesus as the original or primordial sacrament. Again, most of the material on the primordial sacramentality of Jesus himself is found in the writings of the European theologians. A radical change in sacramental theology as envisioned by the liberation theologians needs an ecclesiological and Christological base. This can best be attained, so it would appear, by utilizing the sacramental character of both the Church and Jesus' humanity.

Let me offer here a few illustrations of what this means, which will help clarify the above observations on the limitations of liberation theology. Gustavo Gutierrez, who rightfully is looked upon as the "founder" of liberation theology, describes the movement at great length in his book *Teología de la liberación*. In the latter part of the book, he has a chapter on the Church as a sacrament of history with a subsection on the Eucharist and community. For him the Eucharist is a celebration of community. But his mention of the Eucharist is not pursued at any length; rather he moves on to the wider issues of community. His treatment of the Eucharist is "in passing" and does not provide us with that grounding one would wish. Gutierrez implies rather than develops the ways in which the Eucharist might share in and manifest communal concerns.

Jon Sobrino, in his book *The True Church and the Poor*, makes scant mention of the Eucharist, and again we are left in the dark as to how the Church and the Eucharist, *qua* sacrament, clearly manifest what Church is meant to be. Leonardo Boff, in his now well-advertised book *Church: Charism and Power*, also makes little allusion to the Eucharist, and yet he spends a great deal of space on the issue of base communities.

In this present work Thomas Richstatter picks up on this notion of base community which he calls intentional community and relates it well to the Eucharist. This is the connection that needs to be made again and again: how the social unity, that is, the base community or the intentional community, in all its social dimension is nourished by the Eucharist and in what ways the Eucharist shares in and manifests these very social dynamics of the community. Otherwise, we simply have unreflected and gratuitous statements linking the Eucharist to the social and cultural worlds we actually live in. Such a developed use of the social sciences in relation to the Eucharist is still germinal in many ways, but it is to the credit of many North American scholars that this line of thought is being pursued.

The Ecumenical Understanding of the Sacraments

In the *Decree on Ecumenism* "Unitatis redintegratio," promulgated by the Second Vatican Council, we read:

Catholics must gladly acknowledge and esteem the truly Christian endowments for our common heritage which are to be found among our separated brethren. . . . We must become familiar with the outlook of our separated brethren. Study is absolutely required for this, and it should be pursued in fidelity to the truth and with a spirit of good will. . . . Nevertheless, when they (the separated brethren)

commemorate the Lord's death and resurrection in the Holy Supper,
they profess that it signifies life in communion with Christ and await
his coming in glory.[12]

These are carefully selected words, of course, and to some sound
quite conservative and perhaps timid. On the other hand, when
one realizes that the official attitude of the Roman Catholic Church
since the time of the Reformation has been by and large quite hostile to "our brethren of other Christian confessions," the steps that
the Second Vatican Council has taken can only be judged revolutionary. There is indeed a forthright and strong stance of the Roman
Catholic Church toward the ecumenical movement, and not only
simply in general terms, but also specifically in relation to the Eucharist.

The Eastern Churches offer no difficulty (see *Decree on
Ecumenism*, 14-18), for these Churches possess true sacraments,
above all the priesthood and the Eucharist. In this there has not
been any change of position in the stance of the Western Church
vis-à-vis the Eastern Churches. The forward step of the council consists in the degree of *communicatio in sacris* which the Western
Church now allows.

With regard to Protestant groups, the attitude is startling. At
the heart of the problem is the "absence of the sacrament of Orders."[13] Nonetheless,

> when they commemorate the Lord's death and resurrection in the
> Holy Supper, they profess that it signifies life in communion with
> Christ and await his coming in glory. For these reasons, the doc-
> trine of the Lord's Supper, of the other sacraments, worship and
> ministry in the Church should form subjects of dialogue.[14]

The Lima document on baptism, the Eucharist, and ministry is
but another and more recent indication of the Catholic Church's
positive move toward Eucharistic consensus. The list of ecumenical statements and guidelines dealing with the Eucharist has become
formidable, and all of this indicates that Eucharistic theology today cannot be done except in an ecumenical framework. The emphasis and direction provided by both the Vatican and the national
conferences of bishops in almost every country is quite clear: theologize on the Eucharist in an ecumenical way.

Even the liturgical renewal of the Roman Catholic Church as
far as the Eucharistic liturgy is concerned has been accomplished
with the assistance of and in consultation with major Protestant
scholars. Likewise the liturgical renewal of the Anglican and Lu-

theran communities has been done with the assistance and consultation of Roman Catholic scholars. Thus if one turns to Eucharistic theology, the ecumenical dimension is clearly present.

It is remarkable that in many of the consensus documents and in the requirements for a non-Catholic to receive the Eucharist in the Catholic Church, no mention is made of transubstantiation. Belief in the real presence is requisite, but the "how" of this presence is not a demand. This official stance of the Catholic Church indicates that today one need not hold an intrinsic link between the two. In other words the door is open to alternative theological explanations of the real presence.

What this means to the future is still not clear, however. Since the Eucharist is so interwoven with the sacrament of orders, no clear position is or will be in sight until the issues of Eucharistic presidency have been satisfactorily provided for. Still, as the Lima document readily attests, there have been major forward-looking steps taken on this matter as well. The desire is not to maintain the defensive positions of the Counter-Reformation theologians, but rather to investigate as openly as possible the various interpretations of ministry in the Church. Even the Second Vatican Council provided a fresh beginning on this matter with its rejection of the narrow Scholastic view of priesthood and its endorsement of a more pastoral, apostolic, and christocentric approach. It would be far beyond the scope of this present chapter to move into all the factors involved, but the Lutheran/Catholic dialogues which took place in the United States over the past few years provide one with a classic example of the dynamics and flow involved. The topic of the first dialogue was the Nicene Creed. Little difference between the two Churches was discovered, so the discussants moved to one of the issues in the Nicene Creed: baptism for the remission of sin. Again there was little difference between the Lutherans and the Catholics on the subject. Baptism, however, is the welcoming into the Church and as such into Eucharistic fellowship. Thus the third topic was the Eucharist. The report on this dialogue is extremely informative, and the differences between the two traditions became evident. However, these differences could not be adequately considered without some discussion on the issue of ministry, and hence came about the fourth series of discussions. Even then a major issue arose, namely, the papal ministry, and this led to the fifth and final discussion. Much was accomplished by these dialogues, but perhaps the most noteworthy methodological factor is the interconnection and flow from one topic to the next.

This classic movement of the discussion involving the Eucharist helps us today to see that the ecumenical aspects of Eucharistic theologizing involve much more than simply the Eucharist itself. It also indicates that solutions to many areas of Eucharistic theology cannot be resolved without at the same time facing and at least partially resolving other theological areas as well.

A note might be added here on the issue of the social sciences. Already we have seen that there has been an influence of history on the question of the Eucharist. This has come from biblical history and the history of the sacraments. It has also come from the area of an historicized philosophy, since both existentialism and phenomenology owe much to their historical positioning in modern times. Liberation theology likewise moves from the historical situation of the Church in Latin America today to its own theologizing on the Word of God, a Word which is also heard in the sacraments. Finally, the ecumenical movement comes from our own century and is clearly inculturated in the contemporary movement of the Churches.

History can indeed be seen as one of the social sciences, since it is caught up in psychology, anthropology, and sociology. John Westerhoff in his chapter treats of these social sciences and their effect on the Eucharist, but much more needs to be done. Symbol systems and ritual have much to learn from psychology; the very idea of a community cannot be understood without understanding its sociological and anthropological roots. The influence of a given culture needs to be reexamined. As the Roman Catholic Church moves from a predominantly and dominating European institution to a truly multicultural Church, the social sciences will play an ever more important role. The question always arises as to what to maintain by way of sacred tradition and what can be seen by way of cultural traditions. All societies tend to be conservative and traditional; otherwise, the society begins to lose its very identity. Aspects of social life are not discarded easily; only when one truly understands that what we are "used to" might not be what is "essential" does one see the value of change.

Thomas Kuhn, a well-known contemporary sociologist, speaks of our present age as the third age in world history to undergo a "paradigm change." Paradigms are the keystone ideas that keep a civilization and a culture together. In Western Civilization paradigms changed with the influx of Greek thinking, particularly around the time of Alexander the Great and the Greek domination of the then known Western world. The next true "global" paradigm change came with the arrival of the Germanic tribes from the fifth to the ninth centuries A.D. Only in our present time (last century and our own) is there a new and equally dramatic paradigm shift. Far outside the range of any religious group, the Western world is undergoing a change in the very key ideas which have made its existence cohesive. Science, physics, genetics, psychology, and history, including evolutionary ways of thought, have all contributed to this "new" math of life. Our theology is not perennial, in the sense that it is above such changes. Just as we saw the Hellenization of Christian theology in the early centuries of Church life, and just as we saw a Germanization of canon law and Church structure in the early medieval period—changes which today, far from the battles such changes involved, seem quite acceptable and even divinely shaped— we are presently in the very eye of another hurricane of change, and it is to many discomfiting. Only solid study of the social sciences can bring some rational understanding and acceptance of what is taking place. In the Hellenization and Germanization periods the faith of the Christian community remained exactly what it was always meant to be: the gift of faith, not a rationalized interpretation of God and the world. So, too, today one's faith can indeed remain strong, but it takes more than faith to understand what is happening to a changing world, and above all to a culture enduring "paradigmatic shifts."

We have been used to a view (if not an actuality) of a monolithic or unified Church structure. Base communities and intentional communities seem so localized. John Haughey's contribution to this present study, with its analysis of the local community of Corinth, helps to bring out this aspect of both Church and Eucharistic life. For the community at Corinth it was the "good news" of Paul's preaching that stood at the heart of the group. In the base communities in Latin America today, it is the Gospel which stands at the heart of the group, that is, God's Word calling each member to the very rudiments of Jesus' message. The base community is not primarily a way of structuring a group so that it can operate more efficiently; rather, it is a way of being together so that the community itself can be the Church in a more profound way. The first movement of the base community or the intentional community is the same as that for Corinth. As Haughey indicated, it is a movement inward to the community so that the grouping of people, the gathered flock, can indeed be the Church of God. Nor is there simply a greater awareness of the brotherhood and sisterhood of all who are present (although this is indeed one of the aspects of such communities), but it is an awareness that the Lord is also part of such a community, and not simply there as one among others, but indeed the one who calls the community together. It is, in the Eucharist—the Lord's own supper—not simply a supper where he, too, happens to be a guest. No, he is the one who invites, who serves, and who is himself the nourishment.

In the United States the dominant understanding of the Eucharist has been from the side of the white (middle class and above) North American. Our parishes with their schools and gyms have given us the physical structure for Eucharist. And yet in the early part of this century there were many Roman Catholic churches in which the upper church was for the white and the lower church (the basement) was for the Hispanic. There were churches for the black Catholics and better churches for the white community; early on in this century Asians hardly counted. In this pattern of church and Eucharistic attendance, the theology of the Eucharist was continually developed from that of the dominant white family. Liberation was hardly a factor, although there were subtle ways in which the very church building indicated that Roman Catholics were being liberated from the immigrant past and made part of the melting pot of the American scene. American flags were evident in the sanctuary of the church. Catholics who had become professional were often singled out in many subtle ways. When John Kennedy became President of the United States, Roman Catholics felt that they had arrived on the American cultural scene. A liberation had taken place.

In the aftermath of Martin Luther King's untimely end, a few black Catholic priests were appointed bishops. Again many felt that there was a liberation. The Hispanics on their part have made a more hesitant climb into the ranks of the episcopal hierarchy. Their slow ascendancy was considered as well a sort of liberation. Hispanic men became married deacons. In spite of all this, many things indicated that the North Americans had not really understood what liberation really entailed. Liberation was still quite calculated as liberation to the established Roman Catholic patterns of the white American Church with its strong clerical domination. The bishops of Appalachia spoke out eloquently for the poor in their district, and their letter was splendid. Its impact has been less than expected. Detroit experienced the "Call to Action," and the call is still in so many ways to be heard. Women, particularly religious women, have voiced their sentiments and discontent at an ecclesial second-class citizenship. Small strides only have been taken in this matter. Important as all these issues are—and indeed they are of deep significance—the American Catholic Church is not a Church which by and large feels itself in need of liberation—some sort of dusting off, perhaps, but not a liberation.

The base communities of Latin America, just as the communities of Paul at Corinth, understood liberation more sharply than we do in North America. The reasons for this are clearly theological. At the end of his study on the history of American Catholicism, James Hennesey, S.J., summarized the situation as follows:

> Father Philip J. Murnion of the archdiocesan Office of Pastoral Research commented: "The church, as a community of clear positions, strong leadership and important relationships has been lost somewhere along the way. People do not want 'that old time religion.' They are not asking for retrenchment to rigid rules and clerical dominance. They favor an outreaching church, lay participation, and a revival of a sense of community around faith and mutual caring. They want leadership." A plainer statement of the end of the immigrant phase of American Catholic history could not be made. Whether one looks to the structuring and activities of the ecclesial community, to personal, paraliturgical, or liturgical prayer life, or to the beliefs central to the core of it all, the fundamental challenges facing American Catholics in 1981 are challenges rooted in theology.[15]

These theological challenges still need to be worked through, not only regarding the Eucharist, but also regarding other basic Roman Catholic theological positions.

Bridge to the American Scene

The above framework indicates that Eucharistic theology today is a multidimensional project. It involves tradition, which is a scholarly, nondefensive approach to historical development. This historical development has clearly taken place with the guidance of the Holy Spirit. Still it is history and therefore time-conditioned. The venture also involves solid study of the Bible, particularly the New Testament, which includes the insights that recent biblical criticism has brought to bear on the matter. Third, the role not simply of one philosophy but of various philosophies is highlighted. The Church has never endorsed in an infallible way a given philosophy, so Catholics are free to explore other philosophical stances besides the Scholastic approach. Of serious importance today are the sociological implications of Christian life and teaching. Liberation theology has focused contemporary Eucharistic theology on this sociological framework. Last, the ecumenical movement has been endorsed officially by the Roman Catholic Church, and no Eucharistic theologizing can be done today outside this ecumenical framework without violating the directives of the Second Vatican Council.

Never before in the history of Eucharistic theology has such a convergence of factors played so major a role in the scholarly approach to the subject. This is, therefore, the challenge of our times as regards Eucharistic theology, and this challenge has in many ways revolutionized the American scene.

The Eucharist in the American Church

The American Church experience has revolved in many central ways around the Eucharist. For several reasons, which cannot be explored here, the Catholic groups which migrated to the United States in the 1800s remained in large numbers in the major eastern cities. With a language basis other than English, the Church became the center of worship as well as the center of education (the rise of parochial schools) and social activity (clubs, sodalities, even theater and dance). Not only did the celebration of the Mass remain central, but such devotions as Benediction and Forty Hours took on a major focus for the Christian life. Indeed American Catholics were some of the world's best Catholics as far as Mass attendance on Sunday was concerned. Young boys were urged to be altar boys and even to enter the seminary and study for the priesthood. American Catholicism was rooted in the Eucharist.

The liturgical movement owes much to the Benedictines at St. John's Abbey in Minnesota. These monks published the journal *Orate Fratres*, which today is called *Worship*. Many of the liturgical ideas current in the sacramental renewal of the Second Vatican Council had been prepared for by the American Benedictines. Music in English, prayers in English, an effort to have lay people understand the Mass, these and many other aspects were urged by the monks, and this was in the 1920s, 1930s, and 1940s. It can easily be seen that the American scholar of liturgy was well prepared for the changes of the Second Vatican Council if he or she had kept abreast of the work of these Benedictines.

On the other hand, most of the theologians who taught in the American seminaries and novitiates of religious men and women were themselves taught in Europe, especially in Rome. This meant that until the 1960s most of the theology presented to the American people was European and above all Roman. In the 1960s a new phenomenon occurred. Americans began to study in European centers of theology outside of Rome and returned to the United States with new ideas, ideas which were the center of the Second Vatican Council. The United States gradually could boast of theologians who were "world" scholars. No longer were the great theologians only Europeans. Now, even though slowly, American biblical scholars, American moral theologians, and American dogmatic (systematic) theologians were being quoted and looked up to by world scholarship.

Of singular importance was the relationship of Catholic and Protestant. In some predominantly Catholic countries this relationship is difficult to understand, because the Catholic population by and large does not know any Protestant people. In the United States this is quite different. At the Second Vatican Council the American approach to freedom of religion was finally, after the most heated debates of the council, adopted. The American bishops over the decades had generally been socially very open while theologically more traditional. This two-pronged approach was pragmatic, that is, it worked. The Catholic hierarchy remained very supportive of the rise of the American unions. After all, large numbers of workers came from Catholic immigrant families. Only at the time of the Second Vatican Council and thereafter, with the Church in the United States proudly claiming its own number of American theologians, did these same theologians begin to integrate more carefully social concerns and theological concerns. Prior to this period the American Catholic could struggle for union rights, knowing that bishops and priests backed him or her, but also attend the Eucharist and be nourished on an individual basis. The situation of a Mass being celebrated in a Detroit parking lot to highlight union demands was never thought of in the 1920s, 1930s, 1940s, or 1950s. With the United Farm Workers movement in the 1960s and 1970s, this situation, that is, a mass for union strikers in a Safeway parking lot, did occur. Some bishops found this difficult to mesh with traditional Eucharistic theology. But the question remains: how can American Catholics attend the Eucharist in middle American churches on the one hand and not on the other hand feel the injustice of oppressed groups right here in the United States? All the issues of social concern/Eucharistic theology have not been answered by either Catholic or Protestant American theologians, but the questions are indeed present in our American understanding of Church and sacrament. We cannot wish these questions away, nor can we simply revert to the traditional approach of social issues on the one hand and theology on the other.

Perhaps in no other part of the Christian world has the "women's issue" become as prominent as in the United States. The repercussions are felt strongly both on Eucharistic practice and on Eucharistic theology. The Eucharistic liturgy was exclusively masculine until the Second Vatican Council, that is, priests dominated, only altar *boys* were allowed, women were generally excluded from the sanctuary, and the language of the Mass, at least when translated into English, was masculine. Such a male-oriented practice raised questions about a male-oriented theology. The presence of women who read one of the scriptural passages, who were Eucharistic ministers, who were "altar girls," or who performed such things as liturgical dance caused considerable stir and in many areas still remains a stressful situation. Some women boycott the Eucharistic liturgy; others have protested at ordinations to the priesthood. The questions which this women's issue raises will not go away. Fiats, even from the Vatican, are not effective. Dialogue is necessary and an openness to nontraditional approaches, whenever appropriate, must be present. Indeed the contribution of American women to the Church has been enormous. The parochial school system, Catholic hospitals, much of the Catholic charities programs would never have occurred without the faith, energy, and devotion of American Catholic women. So, too, in our day American Catholic women have raised the issue of the responsible presence of women in decision-making areas and in liturgical celebration. By its very structure the current Eucharistic liturgy "makes a statement." Traditional Eucharistic and priestly theology, as well as an understanding of Church, grounded this masculine approach. If, however, women begin to play a greater role in the decision-making areas of the Church, then they will clearly become more evident in the liturgical celebrations of the people of God.

Dreams of the Future

Can we see in the American position today, as far as Catholics are concerned, the dream of the North American Catholic future? In many ways this is impossible since matters are still quite murky. But there are indeed movements, stemming from our own North American past, which can only move us more into the course of the future which these movements themselves have begun. We do not start with a *tabula rasa.* Already in the 1930s our North American liturgists were strongly social-minded. One need only look to the pioneering efforts of Virgil Michel, O.S.B., Martin Hellriegel, Godfrey Diekmann, O.S.B., and Gerald Ellard, S.J. They sensed that the liturgy, and in particular the Eucharist, was a social activity; accordingly they stressed participation and involvement. Virgil Michel in particular saw that the liturgy and the Eucharist could not be social if Christian life itself were not socially oriented. His ideas of liturgy and Christian living did much to influence some major social movements in the North American Catholic Church at that time: the Catholic Youth Organization, the Christian Family Movement, the Young Christian Workers, and the Young Christian Students. There were as well the Catholic Interracial Council and the Labor Alliance. Catherine de Hueck Friendship Houses and many aspects of the Catholic Worker movement found a theoretical base in Michel's writings. Still the majority of people "went to Mass," and some even "received Communion." Only more recently do we speak of "celebrating the liturgy," or "participating in the Eucharist." Only recently do we discuss such issues as Eucharistic ministers and readers of the Word.

The future will indeed be "social" for Roman Catholics in North America. This does not mean that Eucharists will be forums for social politicking, but rather that the celebration of the Eucharist itself will reflect the multiplicity of peoples, rich and poor, male and female, varied in race, varied in culture. Such a Eucharist cannot be a melting pot Eucharist, as though that were the kind of social oneness the Eucharist speaks of. In such a melting pot Eucharist we are liberated from our backgrounds into the common denominator. We lose ourselves and our rootage. Rather, liberation is the liberation of the entire person with all his or her background and traits. It is the affirmation of the individual person, not in splendid isolation but as partners within the people of God.

Indeed there is a long way to go in this matter, and there will be much more clash of opinions, particularly theological, before clarity begins to show itself.

Footnotes

1. See the English translation in *Rome and the Study of Scripture* (St. Meinrad, Ind.: Abbey Press, 1964) 80–107, especially numbers 35–39.
2. A study on these philosophies can be found in Richard Zahner and Don Ihde, *Phenomenology and Existentialism* (New York: Putnam, 1973).

3. H. C. Lea, *A History of Auricular Confession and Indulgences in the Latin Church* (Philadelphia: Lea Bros., 1896) 3 vols.

4. B. Neunheuser, *Handbuch der Dogmengeschichte* (Freiburg: Herder 1963) vol. 4.

5. J. Betz, *Mysterium Salutis* 4/2 (Einsiedeln: Benziger 1973) 183–314.

6. J. Betz, *Die Eucharistie In der Zeit der Griechischen Väter* (Freiburg: Herder, 1955).

7. J. Jeremias, *The Eucharistic Words of Jesus*, (London: SCM Press) 1966.

8. H. M. Legrand, "The Presidency of the Eucharist According to the Ancient Tradition," *Worship* 53, no. 7 (September 1979) 436.

9. E. Schillebeeckx, *The Eucharist* (New York: Sheed & Ward 1968).

10. J. Segundo, *The Sacraments Today* (New York: Orbis, 1974).

11. *Ibid.* 10.

12. *Decree on Ecumenism*, 4, 9.

13. *Ibid.* 22.

14. *Ibid.*

15. James Hennesey, *American Catholics* (Oxford University Press, 1981) 331.

References

Betz, J. *Die Eucharistie in der Zeit der Griechischen Vaeter.* Freiburg: Herder, 1955; "Eucharistie als Zentrales Mysterium," *Mysterium Salutis*, vol. IV/2, Einsiedeln, Benziger, 1973. Betz provides us with excellent material on the Eucharistic theology of the early Greek Fathers of the Church. Their theological understanding of the Eucharist is different from our Latin, Western theological approach. More emphasis is placed on mystery, on the Holy Spirit, and on the community. All of these emphases were emphasized by the Second Vatican Council as regards Eucharistic liturgy.

Duffy, R. *Real Presence, Worship, Sacraments.* New York: Harper & Row, 1980. A contemporary approach to Eucharistic theology, using existential ways of thinking, phenomenological methods, and a modern approach to symbolism.

Emminghaus, J. *The Eucharist.* Collegeville, Minn.: The Liturgical Press, 1978. Emminghaus presents us with a good overview of the history of the Eucharist in Western ritual and also a fairly lengthy analysis of the liturgy promulgated after the Second Vatican Council.

Guzie, T. *Jesus and the Eucharist.* New York: Paulist Press, 1974. This small book has been very popular, and this is precisely its advantage. However, by being popular it does not offer enough background for a deep understanding of the Eucharist today.

Jeremias, J. *The Eucharistic Words of Jesus.* London: SCM Press, 1966. This is one of the standard contemporary works on the Eucharist, and no serious theological discussion can be done on the Eucharist without using Jeremias' ideas. Some of his conclusions have been upgraded, but the work is by far still substantial.

Kiefer, A. *Blessed and Broken.* Wilmington, Michael Glazier, 1982. This is part of the Glazier series on the sacraments written by a liturgical scholar. The focus is on liturgy and ritual rather than on the theological discussion.

Legrand, H. M. "The Presidency of the Eucharist according to the Ancient Tradition," *Worship*, 53, no. 7 (1979). This article was first published in French, but because of its value, the editors of *Worship* had it translated for an English-speaking audience. The author carefully considers the early material and develops his thesis well. A main issue today is the relationship of Eucharist and ordained ministry. Legrand's work is a solid help to this dialogue.

Neunheuser, B. "Eucharistie in Mittelalter und Neuzeit," *Handbuch der Dogmengeschichte.* Freiburg: Herder, 1963. Neunheuser, one of Europe's major scholars on sacramental theology, presents one of the better surveys of the history of the Eucharist in the Middle Ages and the period after the Council of Trent. He is not concerned with the early Church nor with the contemporary period in any great detail.

Powers, J. *Eucharistic Theology.* New York: Herder & Herder, 1967. This is a dated book, written by a student of Schillebeeckx. There is a broad overview of Eucharistic controversies in the Western Latin Church. Also there is a small but significant bibliography on authors (up to 1966) who had written on the issue of transignification.

Schillebeeckx, E. *The Eucharist.* New York: Sheed & Ward, 1968. This is now a dated book as well but remains a clear expression of (a) the teaching on the Eucharist by the Council of Trent, and (b) the meaning of current ideas on the Eucharist, that is, transignification.

Seasoltz, K. *Living Bread, Saving Cup.* Collegeville, Minn.: The Liturgical Press, 1982. A liturgical study of the Eucharist based on documents.

Swidler, L., ed. *The Eucharist in Ecumenical Dialogue.* New York: Paulist Press, 1976. An intriguing dialogue between Catholic and non-Catholic scholars on the Eucharist. Each author makes an essay and in turn his or her copartner responds. The authors include Kilmartin, Dulles, Hellwig, Osborne, Lindbeck, Aghiorgoussis, Crabtree, and Werner.

W.C.C. (World Council of Churches). *Baptism, Eucharist, and Ministry.* Geneva, W.C.C., 1982. This is called the "Lima Document" and is the result of decades of ecumenical discussion. It touches on all the major aspects of the Eucharist, including those which still cause difficulties between the Christian denominations.

RITUALS

ALTERNATIVE FUTURES FOR THE EUCHARIST

PART I: LITURGY OF THE EUCHARIST

Thomas Richstatter, O.F.M.

Recent History and Projection

Two alternative rites are given here. The first rite is intended for a meeting of a basic community in a home on a weekday; the second rite is for the meeting of the "community of communities," the several basic communities that would form a parish. This second rite is intended for Sundays. The first rite can be adapted to those situations in which there is an ordained priest present and the intentional community wishes to celebrate the Eucharist, and to those occasions where there is no priest present and the community will partake of a meal of fellowship in union with the parish community by sharing consecrated bread and wine brought from a previous Sunday Eucharist.

BACKGROUND TO THE RITES

The rites which are presented here are intended to be a possible ritual expression of the American Church described in the preceding chapters of this book. It is no easy task to describe a future possible Eucharistic ritual, for to do so necessitates a prior vision of a future possible Church. The Eucharist is not only the humble and obedient response to our Lord's command to "Do this in memory of me"; it is also the outstanding way in which a community expresses its self-identity and proclaims to the world a vision of what it means to be Church. The Second Vatican Council describes the liturgy as "the outstanding means whereby the faithful may express in their lives and manifest to others the mystery of Christ and the real nature of the true Church."[1] The essays of this book give a vision of what that future Church might look like.

THE FUTURE CHURCH

"The Church, in Christ, is in the nature of a sacrament—a sign and instrument of communion with God and of unity among all men and women."[2] The shape of the future Church will depend upon the relation and balance of the ways in which this communion and unity are expressed. I find perhaps one of the clearest statements of this balance in article 7 of the *Constitution on the Sacred Liturgy:*

> To accomplish so great a work, Christ is always present in his Church, especially in its liturgical celebrations. He is present in the sacrifice of the Mass, not only in the person of his minister, "the same now offering, through the ministry of priests, who formerly offered himself on the cross," but especially under the eucharistic elements. By his power he is present in the sacraments, so that when a man baptizes it is really Christ himself who baptizes. He is present in his word, since it is he himself who speaks when the holy Scriptures are read in the Church. He is present, lastly, when the Church prays and sings, for he promised: "Where two or three are gathered together in my name, there am I in the midst of them" (Matt 18:20).

The implications of the preceding chapters of this book can be organized in the framework provided in this description of the modes of presence of Christ in his Church, namely, sacrament, minister, Word, and assembly.

The first chapters of this book call for a future alternative Eucharistic rite which would move beyond our preoccupation with sacrament (in a narrow sense of "Eucharistic elements") and minister (in the narrow sense of male, celibate, ordained ministry) and to balance sacrament and minister with Christ's presence in Word and assembly.

SACRAMENT AND MINISTRY BEFORE THE COUNCIL

"Contact with the divinity," "religious experience," "real presence" is fundamental to religion and consequently to worship. Formerly American Catholics found this presence principally in the Eucharistic elements—bread, tabernacle, Mass—and in the priest.

The tabernacle was central to the external architecture of Catholic faith, just as transubstantiation was central to its inner structuring and the consecration and elevation central to its ritual expression. The essential parts of the Mass were offertory, consecration, and communion (as testified to by the fact that to miss these on a Sunday was a *mortal* sin). "Real presence" was what made *us* Catholic and *them* (everybody else) not Catholic.

The priest was "another Christ" (*alter Christus*). He could say "This is *my* Body" and "*I* absolve you from your sins." The image *alter Christus*, which for ten centuries explained what happened to a person at Christian initiation, had become an explanation of what happened at presbyteral ordination.

It is this understanding of sacrament and minister that must be enlarged and brought into balance with Word and assembly.

CHRIST'S PRESENCE IN HIS WORD

"When the holy scriptures are read in the Church, Christ is present, since it is he himself who speaks when the holy scriptures are read."[3] American Catholics have come to grips with the real presence in the liturgical Word quicker than with the real presence in assembly. The *Constitution on the Sacred Liturgy* directed that "the treasures of the Bible are to be opened up more lavishly, so that a richer share of God's word may be provided for the faithful."[4] This article was implemented by the publication of the new three cycle *Lectionary* in 1969.[5] We have had nearly twenty years experience of hearing the Word Sunday after Sunday in our own language. We have seen a corresponding growth in interest in the Bible with study groups, prayer meetings, and groups which read the Scriptures to prepare homilies.

The only point I wish to make here is to draw attention to the fact that Christ's presence in the liturgical Word has taken on an importance in our American Eucharist that it did not have twenty years ago. Ask an American child today what the C.C.D. teacher says are the important parts of the Mass, and instead of "offertory, consecration, and Communion," the answer will most likely be "liturgy of the Word and liturgy of the Eucharist." The very structure of the Eucharistic action has been altered in the popular mind.

As Catholics have grown in their experience of the Word, biblical scholars have continued to examine the meaning of the text. As indicated in the Osborne chapter, there have been numerous studies in our century on the Eucharist in the Scriptures. As our understanding of the Word grows, we are led to modify our understanding of the Eucharist with regard to assembly, minister, and sacrament. Perhaps the most startling development is the balance in understanding Christ's presence in the bread and his presence in the Christian community, which is the focus of the Haughey essay above.

CHRIST'S PRESENCE IN THE ASSEMBLY

"Where two or three are gathered in my name, there am I in their midst" (Matt 18:20). The importance of the assembly as the Body of Christ is going to be the greatest influence on the restructuring of our future Eucharistic rituals.

The attention given to the assembly is growing. One of the most prestigious of all liturgical meetings, the Conference of Saint Serge in Paris, France, chose "Roles in the Liturgical Assembly" as the theme of its 1976 meeting. Papers were given on "The Communal Character of Public Worship," "Assembly and Body of Christ: Identity or Distinction," "The Liturgical Assembly and its Functions," "Is Presbyteral Ordination of the Celebrant a Condition for the Celebration of the Eucharist?" and "The Relation of Priest and Faithful in the Liturgies of Pius V and Paul VI."[6] In 1979, Gerard Austin, O.P., placed this changing understanding of the role of the assembly central to his assessment of American liturgical renewal. In his presidential address to the North American Academy of Liturgy, he stated that our failure to understand the presence of Christ in the assembly and the resulting excessive passivity of the congregation is "our number one problem."[7] In 1981 "The Assembly" was the topic for the National Meeting of Diocesan Liturgical Commissions.

The conclusions of these years of intense discussion on the assembly which are pertinent to our imagining a future Eucharistic ritual can be summarized as follows: (a) the presence of Christ in the Eucharist and his presence in his Body the assembly are seen to be increasingly interrelated (see the Haughey essay above); (b) the focus on assembly gives even greater importance to the analysis of that assembly (see the Westerhoff essay above). A future Eucharistic ritual will, therefore, have to deal with pluralism, the need for intentional communities, the participation of many different people in many different ministries, and most importantly this future ritual will have to balance transubstantiation of the bread and wine with transubstantiation of the assembly. These concerns are central to the rites which follow.

The rites presented here presume that the parish or "community of communities" is composed of smaller intentional communities. The final report of the Parish Project entitled *Parish Life in the United States* indicates that *effective* parishes are three times more likely to have formed miniparishes or subcommunities than the average American parish.[8] "There is much support for the idea that a parish must be seen as a community of communities and of the need to ensure more immediate experience of community in parish life."[9] This is certainly an important factor in projecting a future Eucharistic rite.

MINISTRIES AND CHURCH OFFICES

It is impossible to describe "a possible future Eucharist" without at least imagining "a future possible Church structure and ministry" because the liturgy expresses and manifests the nature of the Church.[10] The future Church is going to have fewer ordained priests; any description of a future Eucharist must take account of this fact. Fewer priests will cause a change in parishes, in the way we view priestly ministry and in the ministries of the faithful, both at the liturgy and in parish life in general. The final report of *Parish Life in the United States* indicates that "it is increasingly likely that there will be but one priest in a parish or, in a growing number of cases, no full-time resident pastor."[11]

While an increasing number of Catholics see the handwriting on the wall, not much seems to be being done to prepare for this situation. An informal study of "Sunday Celebrations Without Priest Presiders" was conducted by the Ministries Committee of the Federation of Diocesan Liturgical Commissions in 1982.[12] Seventy-eight of the 167 dioceses responded to the survey. Some of the questions asked in the survey which are related to the present issue are:

1. Do you have parishes that, because of priest shortages in the past ten years, no longer have resident priests? 33 Yes. 43 No.

2. If the answer to number one was "no," do you foresee this happening in your diocese within the next five years? 14 Yes. 25 No.

3. Is Sunday Mass being celebrated in these parishes that no longer have resident priests? 19 Always. 3 Frequently. 3 Occasionally. 1 Never.

4. At the present time do you have any training program (other than Diaconal) for ministers other than priests who preside at Sunday celebrations? 6 Yes. 71 No.

5. If not, do you see this as a need? 35 Yes, 32 No.

EUCHARISTIC PRAYERS AND THE NONORDAINED

The alternative rites presented here do not try to predict a solution to this difficult problem of what will happen when there are fewer priests. The rite for the Sunday assembly of the community of communities presumes that there will be a priest to proclaim the Eucharistic Prayer. Even the first rite for the weekday celebration by the intentional community is designed for situations where there will be an ordained priest present. The weekday rite, however, also makes provision for situations in which there will be no priest available.

An important question must be faced here: if there is no ordained priest present and the assembly is led by a lay person and there is to be sacramental Communion from bread and wine brought from a previous Sunday parish assembly, should the presider proclaim a prayer of thanksgiving over the already consecrated bread and wine?

Scholars and liturgists are divided on this question. If the nonordained leader of the assembly were to say a prayer of thanksgiving over the already consecrated bread and wine, it is easy to see how people might be confused: the consecratory (Eucharistic) prayer at Mass is essentially a prayer of thanksgiving. The proclamation of such a prayer by a nonordained person at a non-Eucharistic assembly would make the rite appear to be a Mass. On the other hand, praise and thanksgiving (Eucharist) are central to the prayer of every assembly of the faithful. Furthermore, consecration of the elements is not the sole function of the Eucharistic Prayer in the sense that if there is not going to be a consecration, there is nothing for a Eucharistic Prayer to do. The grateful remembering of the saving works of God, the invocation of the Spirit upon the Body of Christ, prayers for unity of believers, and intercession for the whole Church, both the living and the dead, are functions central to the Eucharistic Prayer.

At present different countries have solved the question in different ways. *The Rite of Distributing Holy Communion Outside of Mass with the Celebration of the Word*[13] approved for use in the United States does *not* have a thanksgiving (Eucharistic) prayer. The structure of the rite is as follows:

Introductory Rites
Greeting
Penitential Rite

> Celebration of the Word of God
>
> Holy Communion
> Lord's Prayer
> Sign of Peace
> Invitation
> Communion
> Concluding Prayer
>
> Concluding Rite
> Greeting
> Blessing

The text also carefully notes those prayers which are reserved for ordained ministers (for example, "The Lord be with you," and "May almighty God bless you").

A similar book published by the Western Liturgical Conference of Canada[14] *does* include a thanksgiving prayer. The structure of the service is as follows:

> Introductory Rites
> Penitential Rite
> Opening Prayer
>
> Liturgy of the Word
> Homily
> Apostles' Creed
> General Intercessions
>
> Collection of Offerings
>
> Rite of Thanksgiving
>
> Communion Rite
> Lord's Prayer
> Admonition to Unity
> Ministering the Sacrament
> Prayer after Communion
>
> Concluding Rite
> Blessing
> Dismissal

The rites which follow in this book *do* contain a thanksgiving prayer for these situations. If the model is "meal", the reasoning would seem to indicate that there *should* be a thanksgiving prayer; we give thanks before eating, even when the meal consists of leftovers. In addition, the rites presented here deliberately try to move beyond the present preoccupation with the transformation of the elements in the contemporary Eucharistic Prayers.

The problem is not a small one, and it will not go away. There are those in the Church in Asia who are asking for authorization of lay catechists to preside at the Christian assembly when no priest is present and to proclaim the Eucharistic/consecratory prayer. Such an authorization would cause a basic rethinking of our traditional notion of presbyter, for we practically identify "priest" with "power to consecrate." At the same time Rome is aware that more and more people are going to be deprived of the Eucharist because of the shortage of priests. In the days immediately before the publication of the current Code of Canon Law, while the draft was on the desk of Pope John Paul II, the following paragraph was added to the code:

> If because of lack of a sacred minister or for other grave cause participation in the celebration of the Eucharist is impossible, it is specially recommended that the faithful take part in the liturgy of the word if it is celebrated in the parish church or in another sacred place according to the prescriptions of the diocesan bishop, or engage in prayer for an appropriate amount of time personally or in a family or, as occasion offers, in groups of families.[15]

While the new code recognizes the problem, the text leaves to the imagination liturgical solutions that would be adequate for forming Christian communities in those areas where this situation would continue for an extended period of time.

Ministries and the Alternative Future for the Eucharist

The future alternative Eucharistic rites presented here presume a larger variety of ministries, both liturgical and extraliturgical, than are presently recognized in the Church. In order that these rites might be understandable, or at least imaginable, to the reader, traditional names for the ministries have been retained when possible. Secular titles for ministers used in these rituals indicate a role similar to that which the title indicates in its secular setting, for example, when the rite speaks of a host or hostess, that ministry entails those functions that a host or hostess would perform in an American cultural setting.

Host/Hostess. The Osborne essay, especially the section "The Biblical Renewal of Eucharistic Interpretation," reminds us of the importance of finding our biblical roots for the Eucharist in a Jewish meal, whether paschal or not. In this context the host/hostess figures play an important role. In a contemporary American context they would function not only as we presently envision the tasks of an usher, but their ministry would include all those things which a host or hostess would do in a secular setting: welcome the guests, see to their needs and comfort, prepare the arrangement of the assembly space, provide any needed introductions, receive and care for the food brought for the meal, etc.

Concelebrants. This term designates the ministry of the assembly. In harmony with the official usage in the rites revised by the Second Vatican Council, the term "celebrant" is no longer used in the rubrics to designate the priest. The clear intention of the official books is to stress the reality that it is the assembly which celebrates.

Leader. This minister is the one who would chair the meeting. At the weekday meeting of the intentional community, the role of leader would rotate among the members of the community as modeled in the *comunidades eclesiales de base.* It is not necessary for the leader of the group to be the one who prays in the name of the group. The prayers may be led by the leader, another member of the community, or perhaps by a priest if there is one present.

President. This ministry is envisioned as a more stable ministry than that of leader, which may be operative for only one meeting. A local community would elect one of its members to be president and charge that person with the ongoing oversight of the community. This ministry would be similar to the present-day pastor of the parish or bishop of the diocese. The term president is used because of the style of leadership it indicates in our culture as described in the Westerhoff essay. This person could well be an ordained deacon in our present ecclesial structure.

Lector. The lector or reader is envisioned to be a minister who proclaims the Word of God (reader), is skilled in interpreting the Word to the community (exegete), is occupied with instructing others in the Word (teacher), and is able to continue the story of God's saving work into the life of this present community (historian). The lector could also be the one who would facilitate the shared homily and the basic community's reflection on the Word (as indicated in the Lee essay).

Secretary. Treasurer. Chair of Standing Committee. These ministries would function as their secular American counterparts.

Musician. Little attention is given in the rites which follow to the role of music and ministry of the musicians. This is not because music would not be important in these future alternative rites (quite the contrary!), but because the current documents (especially the statements of the Bishops' Committee on the Liturgy, *Music in Catholic Worship* and *Liturgical Music Today*) adequately describe this ministry. To try to improve on these documents in this chapter would only complicate the rites which follow.

Priest. The present chapter presumes that only an ordained priest is authorized to proclaim the Eucharistic Prayer. Because the Church of the future is apparently going to have fewer priests, the rites proposed here call for many lay ministries.

Bishop. Though not mentioned in the rite, the rites presume the ministry of the bishop, the national conference of bishops, and the global Church. These would provide the necessary training for ministries when this could not be done within the community. These would provide liturgical books for the assembly: a lectionary which would assure a rich selection of readings as called for by the *Constitution on the Sacred Liturgy*, articles 35 and 51, and also provide norms for appropriate adaptation to the needs of local communities while being attentive to both ecumenical concerns and unity with the global Church; a sacramentary which would provide prayers adapted to the liturgical structure, season, and lectionary. Such books would be even more important than at present, for the ministers envisioned in these future rites would not have received the extensive seminary training of present-day priests.

It is not necessary to have this many different ministers to celebrate the rites which follow. The priest could perform the functions of leader, president, reader, exegete, and homilist as he does now. The plurality of ministries suggested here, while somewhat complicated, is subsequent to what was said about the change in the number of ordained clergy and expectations which will be placed on them in the future.

Christ's Presence in His Sacramental Body

This enlarged understanding of ministry together with the increasing awareness of Christ's presence in the liturgical Word and in the assembly forces a rethinking of the fourth mode of real presence taught in article 7 of the *Constitution on the Sacred Liturgy:* Christ's presence in his sacramental Body. The Haughey essay makes clear that our continuing obedience to the command "Do this in memory of me" causes us to search for those ritual actions which make the participants members of the Body of Christ and members of one another. Bluntly put, the Body of Christ on the altar must be brought back into oneness with the Body of Christ in the pew. Our preoccupation with the transubstantiation of the bread must be placed in the context of the transformation (transubstantiation?) of the assembly.

To say that "the individual members of the assembly are so conjoined to the risen Lord that he and they are Christ now" may seem new or even radical to some. But already in the fourth century St. Augustine was reminding his parish: "If then you are the body of Christ and his members, it is your sacrament that reposes on the altar of the Lord. . . . Be what you see and receive what you are.[16] There you are on the table, and there you are in the chalice."[17]

The individualism of American Catholic piety in the past, as described in both the Westerhoff and Osborne essays, must be surpassed by a rite which makes it immediately obvious that becoming one with Christ and becoming one with one another are the two meanings of one action, as demanded by the Haughey essay. True the bread becomes the Body of Christ, but the Christ who is *now*. To become one with Christ is to become members of an *us*.

To propose an alternative Eucharistic rite which hopefully accomplishes this presence of Christ in bread and assembly, Word and minister, is not to imply that these ends are neglected in the Order of Mass proposed by Vatican II. The current Order of Mass accomplishes these ends in a way far superior to the rite of Trent. It is perhaps for this reason—namely, that the implications of participation are more obvious to the concelebrants than formerly—more than for reasons of change of language or alleged loss of mystery, that some shy away from the current rite. The current rite makes more clear than the rite of Trent that, as John Haughey phrases it, the Eucharist is dangerous food to eat because it makes its consumers what they eat. And that "what they eat" died on a cross. Perilous business indeed! The future alternative rites presented here are hopefully even more dangerous in that regard.

There is no obvious way to achieve this end. I have tried to do so by two means: first, the structure of the rite, and second, the content of the prayers.

The Structure of the Rite. The Haughey essay concludes by stating that "we do not need to devise alternative forms of worship, but that we need to worship according to the alternative we have become in Christ." The rites which follow attempt to be true to this directive. They are not new rites; they are a restructuring of our present rite in such a way that who we have become in Christ is more clearly celebrated.

The rite itself must assist the building up of community. The concelebrants must become more aware of and concerned for one another. More than that, their concern must move beyond the assembly to the community at large and indeed the world. In order to be truly a basic community, there must be outreach beyond the members of the community. As John Haughey stated in his essay, in order for the Mass to be a sign of unity, there has to be a community resulting from it, a community of human beings whose relationship with one another is such that the neutral observer can notice and judge their bondedness.

I have tried to do this not only by the multiplicity and redefinition of ministries but by the addition of a rite of "Inserting Our History into Our World" after the readings ("Entering the Community History"). To some this may seem that the Eucharistic assembly is being interrupted at this point to hold a parish council meeting or that the most sacred action of the Mass is diffused by politics and secular issues. This is not the case. As Regis Duffy has forcefully explained in *Real Presence*, religious commitment "cannot be divorced from the stages of our lives, the work that we do, and the friends that we cherish. When speaking of religious commitment, there are no 'secular' areas of life. For it is in the practical contexts of our lives that we discern our real understandings of faith and sacrament, of service and of church."[18]

The Content of the Prayers. The prayers of the proposed alternative rite attempt to focus attention on the invocation of the Spirit, not only on the gifts to transform them but upon the assembly that they be transformed into the Body. The prayers tend to move away from preoccupation with consecration to expressions of the "new thing" God is creating in us through this ritual celebration. As we try to come into consciousness of what that is, our prayers and our consciousness are often halting and incomplete.

Footnotes

1. Constitution on the Sacred Liturgy (*Sacrosanctum concilium*) article 2.
2. Dogmatic Constitution on the Church (*Lumen gentium*) article 1.
3. Constitution on the Sacred Liturgy, article 7.
4. Article 51. The more general directive referring not only to the Eucharist but all the sacraments is found in article 35,1: "In sacred celebrations there is to be more reading from holy Scripture and it is to be more varied and apposite."

5. Sacra Congregatio pro Cultu Divino. *Ordo Lectionum Missae.* May 25, 1969.

6. J. J. von Allmen, et al. *Roles in the Liturgical Asembly: The Twenty-third Liturgical Conference Saint Serge* (New York: Pueblo, 1981).

7. *Worship* 53:4, 291–301. See especially 296.

8. The Parish Project. *Parish Project in the United States: Final Report to the Bishops of the United States by the Parish Project.* Publication no. 876 (Washington: United States Catholic Conference, 1982) 30.

9. *Ibid* 24.

10. Constitution on the Sacred Liturgy, article 2.

11. *Parish Life in the United States*, 34–35.

12. F.D.L.C. *Newsletter* (September–October 1981) 9:5, 5.

13. International Committee on English in the Liturgy, Inc. *Holy Communion and Worship of the Eucharist Outside of Mass.* Publication no. 886 (Washington: United States Catholic Conference, 1983).

14. *God's Word—Thanksgiving—Communion with Laypersons Presiding* (Regina, Saskatchewan: Western Liturgical Conference of Canada, 1981).

15. Canon 1248,2. The Canon Law Society of America's *Commentary* on the Code says: "The second paragraph of this canon is new and was added immediately before the publication of the Code. It reflects a new and contemporary situation in certain parts of the Church—a situation which will become more acute in the years ahead."

16. Sermon 272.

17. Sermon 229.

18. Regis Duffy. *Real Presence: Worship, Sacraments, and Commitment* (Harper, 1982) 1–2.

Structures and Elements of the Alternative Rites

RITE 1: WEEKDAY ASSEMBLY OF AN INTENTIONAL COMMUNITY

Part I: Gathering
  Welcome
  Community Greeting
  Call to Order
  Opening Prayer

Part II: Proclaiming and Receiving the Word
  Entering the Community History
    Proclamation of the Word
    Exegesis of the Word

Inserting Our History into Our World
   Application of the Word
   Committee Reports
   Homily
   (Sacramental Actions)
   General Intercessions
   Collection
   Decision

Part III: Giving Thanks and Pledging Communion
A. Preparation
   Form 1: Ordained Presider
      Reconciliation
      Lord's Prayer
      Sign of Peace
      Presentation of the Gifts
   Form 2: Nonordained Presider
      Reconciliation
      Lord's Prayer
      Sign of Peace
B. Prayer of Praise and Thanksgiving
   Form 1: Ordained Presider
   Form 2: Nonordained Presider
C. Pledging Our Communion in the Sacred Meal
   Communion
   Prayer after Communion

Part IV: Sending Forth
Announcements
Blessing
Dismissal

Rite 2: Sunday Assembly of a Parish of Intentional Communities

Part I: Gathering
Welcome
Community Greeting
Opening Hymn
Greeting
Opening Prayer

Part II: Proclaiming and Receiving the Word
    Entering the Community History
        Proclamation of the Word
    Inserting Our History into Our World
        Application of the Word:
            Community Reflection
            Group Reflection
        Song
        Homily
        (Sacramental Actions)
        Committee Reports
        General Intercessions
            Community Intentions
            Group Intentions
        Decision

Part III: Giving Thanks and Pledging Communion
    A. Preparation
        Reconciliation
        Lord's Prayer
        Sign of Peace
        Presentation of the Gifts
    B. Prayer of Praise and Thanksgiving
    C. Pledging Our Communion in the Sacred Meal
        Communion
        Prayer After Communion
            Oration
            Group Prayer
            Silent Prayer
            Closing Prayer

Part IV: Sending Forth
    Announcements
    Blessing
    Dismissal
    Closing Hymn

RITE 1: WEEKDAY ASSEMBLY OF AN INTENTIONAL COMMUNITY

TIME AND PLACE

The members of the intentional community gather at the time and place determined at the previous assembly.

ENVIRONMENT

A table is located in the midst of the assembly. Designated members of the community provide the bread and wine for the Eucharistic meal. A bread basket, cup, and any other table settings appropriate to the community are made ready in advance.

TEXTS

The prayer texts suggested here are only generic samples. In an actual celebration, ministers would be guided in composing suitable prayers by: (a) the circumstances of the community, (b) the liturgical occasion and/or season, (c) the liturgical books of the larger Church: diocesan, national or global. The selection of readings would be aided by the larger Church's provision of a lectionary which would: (a) assure the rich selection of readings called for by the Constitution on the Sacred Liturgy, articles 35, 51, (b) provide norms for appropriate adaptation to the needs of the local community.

PART I: GATHERING

The purpose of these rites of gathering is to enable the individual members of the group to form a worshipping community so that, as Church, they may enter into dialogue with the Word of God.

WELCOME

Members are met and welcomed by the *host/hostess* and introduced to anyone they may not know.

COMMUNITY GREETING

The members enter into individual conversations with the others present, greeting one another, catching up on one another's news, welcoming new members personally, and conducting preliminary business pertaining to the assembly. Each person attempts to speak to each other person present. When this part of the rite is completed,

each member has a sense of other members' faith journey as it has
developed since the last meeting.

CALL TO ORDER

When the community greeting has been completed, the *host/hostess:*
—formally welcomes the assembly;
—introduces new members by name;
—recalls particular concerns or intentions for prayer at this
assembly;
—introduces the *leader.*

OPENING PRAYER

Leader: O God and Father of our Savior Jesus Chirst,
look upon our assembly
as we gather in the name of your Son.
He promised to be present
where two or three gather in his name
even as we do now.

We pray that his Spirit so transform us into his
Body
that we may listen to your Word with his ears
and take action with his wisdom and courage.

Be attentive to our simple prayer,
and hear in our hesitant words the voice of your
Son,
our Lord Jesus Christ,
who lives with you and the Holy Spirit,
one God, for ever and ever.

All: Amen.

PART II: PROCLAIMING AND RECEIVING THE WORD

Entering the Community History

PROCLAMATION OF THE WORD

The *lector:*
—announces the Scripture passages which will be the focus of
this meeting; ordinarily the Gospel selected for the next meeting of the Sunday parish assembly is read first;
—proclaims the texts for all to hear.

Exegesis of the Word

The *lector* explains the original context of the texts and answers questions about their meaning.

Inserting Our History into Our World

Application of the Word

Appropriate ministers guide the community's reflection and conversation from the meaning of the text in the context in which it was first formulated to its meaning for hearers in the contemporary context.

The *leader* conducts the conversation toward the text's application to:
—individuals and their households or families;
—this assembly as community of responsibility;
—the geopolitical area: city, district, country.

Committee Reports

The *leader* or the *community president* guides the conversation to areas of specific concern to this assembly, beginning with the community's five standing committees: (a) stewardship and finance, (b) education, (c) community interaction and social life, (d) community outreach for peace and justice, (e) worship and prayer. The activities of the community and its committees are reported and examined in the light of the readings.

Homily

The *leader* either gives a homily or designates another minister (*president, ordained priest, deacon,* or *prophet,* i.e., a community member with the gift of preaching) to do so. The purpose of the homily is to enable the Word once spoken in the apostolic context to be spoken now to this community and to become effective in such wise that the community may know that Christ "is present in his word, since it is he himself who speaks when the holy Scriptures are read in the Church" (*Constitution on the Sacred Liturgy,* article 7).

Sacramental Actions

If there are any sacramental actions proper to this assembly (scrutinies, healings, institutions, etc.), they take place at this point. Sacramental actions related to the structure of the whole local church (initiations, weddings, ordinations, etc.) ordinarily take place during the larger Sunday assembly.

GENERAL INTERCESSIONS

Leader: My friends,
             once again we have heard the voice of our Savior
             inviting us to respond to his holy Word.
             The diversity of our opinions and resolutions
                   shows us
             not only the wonderful diversity of the Spirit
             but also the woeful limits of our darkened vision.

             Let us ask the God of our Lord Jesus Christ
             to enlighten us with that Spirit
             who clarifies our needs and teaches us to pray.
             Without that Spirit we do not know for what to
                   beg.
             In that Spirit we make known our petitions with
                   confidence.

The *secretary* announces the needs for which the community prays. (Note that all petitions, including those for the Church and its leadership, are stated here rather than in the Eucharistic Prayer.)

At the conclusion of the petitions:

Leader: Most high, all good and glorious God,
             attend to these our halting prayers.
             Open our ears to that voice which is truth.
             Illumine our eyes to see your way.
             Enliven our stony hearts
             that our weary arms might strain
             for the justice which is the glory
             of the kingdom of your Son
             Jesus the Christ
             who rules with you in the unity of the Spirit
             for ever and ever.

All: Amen.

COLLECTION

The *treasurer*, chair of the stewardship committee, directs the collection of money and goods. The *treasurer* reports the community's assets, the amount of the last collection, and the use to which the money was put. The chairpersons of the other standing committees report their stewardship and needs.

Decision

If a priest is present, the *leader*:
  —announces the presence of this ordained priest authorized by the larger community to preside over the celebration of the Eucharist;
  —acknowledges the presence of differences within the community as revealed by the earlier conversations and discernment;
  —asks whether there is sufficient unity among them to allow them to break bread together as members of one Body;
  —determines the mind of the community on this point;
  —either turns the meeting over to the priest, who proceeds with the Eucharistic meal as described below (Form 1), or moves to the prayers of reconciliation and the dismissal.

If no priest is present, the *leader*:
  —announces the presence of N., the acolyte, who has brought bread and wine from the previous Sunday's assembly at the Church of N.;
  —acknowledges the presence of differences within the community as revealed by the earlier conversations and discernment;
  —asks whether there is sufficient unity among them to allow them to break bread together as members of one Body;
  —determines the mind of the community on this point;
  —either continues with the eucharistic texts below (Form 2) or moves to the prayers of reconciliation and the dismissal.

PART III: GIVING THANKS AND PLEDGING COMMUNION

A. Preparation

Form 1

This form is used when an ordained priest presides.

Reconciliation

Priest: Thank you for inviting me to break bread with you and to word your sacred action.
This is a serious request:
anyone who eats the bread or drinks the cup
without recognizing the Body
eats and drinks not blessing but judgment.
Examine yourselves, brothers and sisters.
Are you ready in your flesh
to die to sin and selfishness

that in your body you may proclaim
the death of the Lord until he comes
and pledge the covenant
in the breaking of the bread
and the sharing of the cup?

All: We are.

All join hands.

Priest: My brothers and sisters,
we are about to set the table
and proclaim in our holy meal
the death of the Lord until he comes.

He has cautioned us
that when we bring our gift to the altar
if our brother or sister has anything against us
we must leave our gift
and first cleanse our hands for the giving.
Pray that the Lord create a clean heart in us.

Almighty and merciful God,
let us know your will.

All: R̸. Your kingdom come, your will be done.

Priest: Look not upon our sins but upon our faith. R̸.

Cover us with your peace. R̸.

Let your justice reach to the ends of the earth. R̸.

Heal all divisions among us. R̸.

Lord Jesus, forgive us if we have not fed you.

All: R̸. Forgive us our sins as we forgive those who sin
against us.

Priest: Lord Jesus, forgive us if we have not clothed you. R̸.

Lord Jesus, forgive us if we have not visited you. R̸.

Lord Jesus, forgive us if we have not trusted you.
R̸.

LORD'S PRAYER

Brothers and sisters,
let us pray in the Spirit
even as we have been taught to pray:

All: Our Father . . . .

SIGN OF PEACE

The *priest* invites the assembly to give one another a sign of forgiveness and peace:

Priest: May the peace of the risen Lord be with you
always.

All: And also with you.

After the community has exchanged the sign of peace:

Priest: May almighty God have mercy on us
and forgive our sin.
May our hearts burn with recognition of his Body
as we prepare to break this bread.

PRESENTATION OF THE GIFTS

The community members who have brought the loaf of bread and the bottle of wine for the meal bring them to the *priest* who places them on the table.

Form 2

This form is used when a nonordained minister presides.

RECONCILIATION

Leader: My sisters and brothers,
by breaking anew this bread from our Sunday
Eucharist
and sharing in this cup of blessing
we place ourselves once again in solidarity
with the women and men of the assembly
who first broke this bread and blessed this cup.
One Body with them,
if we now eat and drink with them again
we are responsible for the covenant
which we sealed together then in our communion.
Anyone who eats the bread or drinks of the cup
without recognizing the Body
eats and drinks not blessing but judgment.

Examine yourselves, brothers and sisters.
Are you ready in your flesh

to die to sin and selfishness
that in your body you may proclaim
the death of the Lord until he comes
and pledge the covenant
in the breaking of the bread
and the sharing of the cup?

All: We are.

The consecrated bread and wine are brought to the table.
All join hands.

Leader: My brothers and sisters,
we join hands in the presence
of the sacrament of our reconciliation
to God and to one another.
In our communion with Love itself
every sin and division is overcome,
and we, though many, are made one Body
as we receive the one bread.

Pray that the Lord free us
from all that separates us from God and from one
    another
that we may partake of this sacrament of unity
with one mind and one heart
and in one Spirit.

Almighty and merciful God,
let us know your will.

All: R̷. Your kingdom come, your will be done.

Leader: Look not upon our sins but upon our faith. R̷.

Cover us with your peace. R̷.

Let your justice reach to the ends of the earth. R̷.

Heal all divisions among us. R̷.

Lord Jesus, forgive us if we have not fed you.

All: R̷. Forgive us our sins as we forgive those who sin
against us.

Leader: Lord Jesus, forgive us if we have not clothed you. R̷.

Lord Jesus, forgive us if we have not visited you. R̷.

Lord Jesus, forgive us if we have not trusted you.
R̷.

LORD'S PRAYER

> Brothers and sisters,
> let us pray in the Spirit
> even as we have been taught to pray.

All: Our Father . . . .

SIGN OF PEACE

> The *leader* invites the assembly to give one another a sign of forgiveness and peace:

Leader: Let those who would partake of the sacrament of
> unity
> give sign that they are at peace with his Body.

> After the community has exchanged the sign of peace:

Leader: May almighty God have mercy on us
> and forgive our sin.
> May our hearts burn with recognition of his Body
> as we prepare to break this bread and share this
> cup.

B. Prayer of Praise and Thanksgiving

Form 1

> This form is used when an ordained priest presides.

Priest (in the name of all):

> Father, we thank you.
> What more dare we say?
> We praise you and we bless you.
> Your every act is sacrament
> of your covenant love for us.

All: R̷. Bless us, Lord, and these your gifts.

Priest: Your love is revealed in your Son
> who . . .
> (Here give thanks for the gospel mystery proclaimed
> earlier in the meeting: for example, "restored sight to the
> man born blind and continues to give sight to our blindness
> that we may see your plan and recognize him in
> the breaking of the bread.")
> R̷.

Almighty God,
we are not worthy to name you.
It is only your Spirit who gives us confidence
and makes us bold to come before you.
In this Spirit we have confidence
to do as your Son commanded us to do in his
memory. R̊.

We take bread and give you thanks.
We break the bread and say:
this is my Body. R̊.

We take a cup of wine and give you thanks.
We share the cup among us and drink
the new and everlasting covenant:
blood poured out for sin's forgiveness. R̊.

As we eat the one bread and share the one cup
may your Spirit make us one Body
to proclaim the death of the Lord
until he comes again in that glory
which reveals the fullness of the kingdom
where through him, in him, and with him,
in the unity of the Spirit and your holy Church,
all glory and honor is yours, almighty Father,
for ever and ever.

All: Amen.

Form 2

This form is used when a nonordained minister presides.

Leader (in the name of all):

Father, we thank you.
What more dare we say?
We praise you and we bless you.
Your every act is sacrament
of your covenant love for us.

All: R̊. Bless us, Lord, and these your gifts.

Leader: Your love is revealed in your Son.
We thank you for your revelation in him.
We thank you that he . . .
(Here give thanks for the Gospel mystery proclaimed
earlier in the meeting: for example,

"restored sight to the man born blind
and continues to give sight to our blindness
so that we may see your plan for us
and recognize him as we share this sacred food.")
R̸.

Your love is revealed in our day
and we see your works . . . .
(Here give thanks for the blessings of this community.
The *leader* may invite community members to add their
own motives for thanksgiving: for example,
"We see your love in the healing of Robert's daughter."
"We see your love in the passage of the refugee act.")
For all your gracious gifts we bless you. R̸.

We are not worthy to name you.
It is only your Spirit who gives us confidence
and makes us bold to come before you.
In this Spirit we dare
to take the bread of life
and the cup of salvation. R̸.

As we eat the one bread and share the one cup
may your Spirit make us one Body
to proclaim the death of the Lord
until he comes again in that glory
which reveals the fullness of the kingdom
where through him, in him, and with him,
in the unity of that same Spirit
and in your holy Church,
all glory and honor is yours, almighty Father,
for ever and ever.

All: Amen.

C. Pledging our Communion in the Sacred Meal

This form is used by ordained and nonordained presiders.

COMMUNION

The *presider* shows the bread and wine to the assembly, saying:

Presider: Holy things for God's holy people.

All: Happy are we to be invited to this supper.

The *presider* breaks the loaf of bread in two, saying:

Presider: And they recognized him in the breaking of the bread.

The *presider* gives the bread to the assembly members to the right and to the left, saying:

Presider: The Body of Christ.

Communicant: Amen.

The communicant breaks off a piece of the bread, keeps the fragment in hand, and passes the rest of the loaf to the next communicant, saying: "The Body of Christ." When all have been served, they eat together.

The *presider* gives the cup to the communicant on the right, saying:

Presider: The Blood of Christ.

Communicant: Amen.

The communicant drinks from the cup and passes it to the next communicant, saying: "The Blood of Christ." The cup is thus shared throughout the assembly.

While the cup is passed, a psalm or hymn may be sung or prayers recited.

The empty bread basket and cup are put aside.

PRAYER AFTER COMMUNION

Presider: God of light,
may the celebration of the mysteries of your
  presence
strengthen us to be the Body of your Son,
Jesus the Christ.

All: Amen.

The *leader* invites others who would like to do so to pray aloud and then gives time for silent prayer. If not presiding, the *leader* invites the *presider* to conclude the eucharist.

Presider: Almighty God,
our assembly comes to an end.
Hear these prayers which are uttered
in the name and Spirit of your Son, Jesus Christ,
who rules for ever and ever.

All: Amen.

PART IV: SENDING FORTH

ANNOUNCEMENTS

The *secretary* announces any necessary reminders. The *host/hostess* for the next assembly gives the time, date, and directions for the next meeting.

BLESSING

Presider: Father, Son, and Holy Spirit:
bless us;
keep us in your care;
turn your face to us and have mercy upon us.
Father, Son, and Holy Spirit:
blessed be your name forever!

All: Blessed be God for ever!

DISMISSAL

Leader: Go in peace,
strengthened by Word and bread
for the service of all.
Be what you have seen;
proclaim who you are
that they may say of us
even as they said of our ancestors:
"See how they love one another."
God be with you.

The *host/hostess* bids farewell.

RITE 2: SUNDAY ASSEMBLY OF A PARISH OF INTENTIONAL COMMUNITIES

TIME

The original day for this gathering is the first day of the week, the day of the resurrection of the Lord. Only grave difficulties or cultural obstacles would cause the community to assemble on a different day.

ENVIRONMENT

The community gathers in a place large enough for an appropriate number of intentional communities. The worship space is designed to include a principal table at which the *pastor* presides, surrounded by additional tables for the rest of the assembly. The chairs are arranged so that the concelebrants can attend to the ritual at their table and also that at the head table.

TEXTS

The prayer texts suggested here are only generic samples. In an actual celebration, ministers would be guided in composing suitable prayers by: (a) the circumstances of the community, (b) the liturgical occasion and/or season, (c) the liturgical books of the larger Church: diocesan, national, or global. The selection of readings would be aided by the larger Church's provision of a lectionary which would: (a) assure the rich selection of readings called for by the Constitution on the Sacred Liturgy, articles 35, 51, (b) provide norms for appropriate adaptation to the needs of the local community.

ASSEMBLY

The participants are members of intentional communities accustomed to using Rite 1 (above) for their weekday gatherings. The presider is the pastor of the parish, ordinarily an ordained priest. If the pastor is not ordained, the rite is adapted following the pattern given in Rite 1. The leader could be a deacon or the elected president of the parish. In any case, the leadership of this assembly is different from that of the weekday assembly, in which leadership could rotate among the members.

PART I: GATHERING

The purpose of the rites of gathering is to form in a visible way the Body of Christ from the different members of the assembling intentional communities. In order for this to be accomplished, each member of the community must be helped to enter into both the tradition of the community and the present moment of that tradition as lived in the members gathered.

WELCOME

Members are met and welcomed when they arrive by the *host/hostess* and introduced to anyone they may not know.

The *secretaries* move among the assembling members to learn of any particular needs of the various members of the community, especially those which affect the whole assembly.

COMMUNITY GREETING

The members enter into individual conversations with the others present, greeting one another, catching up with one another's news, welcoming new members personally, and conducting preliminary business pertaining to the assembly. All of the members of each intentional community try to speak to one another. Thus when this part of the rite is completed, each member of the group has a sense of the other members' faith journey as it has developed since the last meeting.

OPENING HYMN

When all have gathered and greeted one another, an appropriate hymn is sung.

GREETING

Pastor (in these or similar words):

> Greetings to the Church of N.
> To you who have been consecrated in Christ Jesus
> and called to be a holy people,
> grace and peace from God our Father
> and the Lord Jesus Christ.

All: Grace and peace be with you.

The *secretary:*
- *—formally welcomes the assembly*
- *—introduces new members by name;*
- *—announces any major community concerns;*
- *—introduces the presider if other than the local pastor.*

OPENING PRAYER

Pastor: O God and Father of our Savior Jesus Christ,
look upon our assembly
as we gather in the name of your Son.
He promised to be present
where two or three gather in his name
even as we do now.

We pray that his Spirit so transform us into his
    Body

that we may listen to your Word with his ears
and take action with his wisdom and courage.

Be attentive to our simple prayer,
and hear in our hesitant words the voice of your
    Son,
our Lord Jesus Christ,
who lives with you and the Holy Spirit,
one God, for ever and ever.

All: Amen.

PART II: PROCLAIMING AND RECEIVING THE WORD

Entering the Community History

PROCLAMATION OF THE WORD

The *lector:*
—designates the passages of Scripture which will be the focus
of this meeting. Ordinarily, they are the passages assigned to
the day by the larger Church in its lectionary;
—proclaims the principal text for all to hear;
—ordinarily does *not* offer an exegesis because those present have
studied the passages in their intentional communities.

Inserting Our History into Our World

APPLICATION OF THE WORD

Appropriate ministers guide the community's reflection and conversation from the meaning of the text in the context in which it was
first formulated to its meaning for hearers in the contemporary
context.

The *pastor* conducts the conversation toward the text's application
to:
—individuals and their households or families;
—this assembly as community of responsibility;
—the geopolitical area: city, district, country.

At each table a *group leader* guides the reflection.
—At some tables, the *group leader* will direct a *lector* in the group
to proclaim other complementary Scripture texts.
—the *group leader* directs the conversation to areas of specific
concern to the group.
—the *group leader* then moves the group to reflect on the needs
of the larger community in light of the readings. Attention is

directed first to the community's five standing committees: (a) stewardship and finance, (b) education, (c) community interaction and social life, (d) community outreach for peace and justice, (e) worship and prayer. The activities of the community and its committees are examined in the light of the readings.

Song

The *pastor* determines the length of this discussion and then asks the *music minister* to begin a chant; for example, "alleluia." This chant is taken up and repeated by each group as they finish their reflection until all the groups are singing together. They then turn their attention to the head table.

Homily

The *pastor* either gives a homily or designates another minister to do so. The purpose of the homily is to enable the Word once spoken in the apostolic context to be spoken now to this community and to become effective in such wise that the community may know that Christ "is present in his word, since it is he himself who speaks when the holy Scriptures are read in the Church" (*Constitution on the Sacred Liturgy*, article 7).

Sacramental Actions

If there are any sacramental actions which reflect the structure and purpose of the whole community (e.g., initiations, weddings, ordinations), they take place at this time.

Committee Reports

The *chairperson* of each standing committee reports to the whole community a summary of their programs in order to draw the community's attention to those matters and persons in need of prayer.

General Intercessions

Pastor: My friends,
once again we have heard the voice of our Savior inviting us to respond to his holy Word.

Let us ask the God of our Lord Jesus Christ
to enlighten us with the Spirit
who clarifies our needs and teaches us to pray.
Without that Spirit we do not know for what to ask.

> In that Spirit we make known our petitions with
> confidence.

The *secretary* announces the needs for which the community prays.
(Note that all petitions, including those for the Church and its leadership, are stated here rather than in the Eucharistic Prayer.)

The *pastor* asks each of the groups to name their needs. The *group
leaders* guide the intercessions within each group.

At the conclusion of the petitions:

Pastor: Most high, all good and glorious God,
attend to these our halting prayers.
Open our ears to that voice which is truth.
Illumine our eyes to see your way.
Enliven our stony hearts
that our weary arms might strain
for the justice which is the glory
of the kingdom of your Son
Jesus the Christ
who rules with you in the unity of the Spirit
for ever and ever.

All: Amen.

COLLECTION

The *treasurer*, chair of the stewardship committee, then directs the
collection of money and goods. The collection takes place in each
of the groups and is brought to the head table.

The *treasurer* reports the community's assets, the amount of the last
collection and the use to which the money was put. The chairpersons of the other standing committees indicate their needs and
stewardship.

DECISION

The *pastor:*

—acknowledges the presence of differences in the community;
—asks whether the assembly believes itself to be sufficiently
united to break bread together as members of one Body;
—determines the mind of assembly on the matter;
—either continues with the Eucharist as described below or moves
to the prayers of reconciliation and the dismissal.

PART III: GIVING THANKS AND PLEDGING COMMUNION

A. Preparation

RECONCILIATION

Pastor: Thank you for inviting me to word your sacred
action
and to lead you in the breaking of the bread.
This is a serious request:
anyone who eats the bread or drinks the cup
without recognizing the Body
eats and drinks not blessing but judgment.
Examine yourselves, brothers and sisters.
Are you ready in your flesh
to die to sin and selfishness
that in your body you may proclaim
the death of the Lord until he comes
and pledge the covenant
in the breaking of the bread
and the sharing of the cup?

All: We are.

The members of each group join hands.

Pastor: My brothers and sisters,
we are about to set the table
and proclaim in our holy meal
the death of the Lord until he comes.
He has cautioned us
that when we bring our gift to the altar
if our brother or sister has anything against us
we must leave our gift
and first cleanse our hands for the giving.
Pray that the Lord create a clean heart within us.

Almighty and merciful God,
let us know your will.

All: R⁊. Your kingdom come, your will be done.

Pastor: Look not upon our sins but upon our faith. R⁊.
Cover us with your peace. R⁊.
Let your justice reach to the ends of the earth. R⁊.

Heal all divisions among us. R̷.

Lord Jesus, forgive us if we have not fed you.

All: R̷. Forgive us our sins as we forgive those who
sin against us.

Pastor: Lord Jesus, forgive us if we have not clothed you. R̷.

Lord Jesus, forgive us if we have not visited you. R̷.

Lord Jesus, forgive us if we have not trusted you. R̷.

The *group leaders* continue this form of prayer in each group as the
prayer for reconciliation is personalized at each table.

The *music minister* intones a chant asking for God's pardon, and
the groups conclude their prayer and enter into the singing.

Lord's Prayer

Pastor: Brothers and sisters,
let us pray in the Spirit
even as we have been taught to pray:

All: Our Father . . . .

Sign of Peace

The *pastor* invites the assembly to give one another a sign of forgiveness and peace:

Pastor: May the peace of the risen Lord be with you always.

All: And also with you.

After each group has exchanged the sign of peace:

Priest: May almighty God have mercy on us
and forgive our sins.
May our hearts burn with recognition of his Body
as we prepare to break this bread.

Presentation of the Gifts

The members of the intentional communities who have brought
loaves of bread and bottles of wine for the meal give them to the
group leaders who place them on the group's table. Sufficient bread
and wine is taken to the head table for the needs of that group.

B. Prayer of Praise and Thanksgiving

Pastor (in the name of all):

> Father, we thank you.
> What more dare we say?
> We praise you and we bless you.
> Your every act is sacrament
> of your covenant love for us.

All: R̍. Bless us, Lord, and these your gifts.

Priest: Your love is revealed in your Son
> who . . .
> (Here give thanks for the gospel mystery proclaimed
> earlier in the meeting: for example, "restored sight to
> the man born blind and continues to give sight to our
> blindness that we may see your plan and recognize him
> in the breaking of the bread.")
> R̍.

The *group leaders* continue this style of prayer at each table, where
group members are given the opportunity to mention motives for
praise and thanksgiving.

At a signal from the *pastor*, the *music minister* begins a chant of
praise and draws the community's attention to the head table.

Pastor: Almighty God,
> we are not worthy to name you.
> It is only your Spirit who gives us confidence
> and makes us bold to come before you.
> In this Spirit we dare
> to do as your Son commanded us to do in his
>   memory. R̍.

> We take bread and give you thanks.
> We break the bread and say:
> this is my Body. R̍.

> We take a cup of wine and give you thanks.
> We share the cup among us and drink
> the new and everlasting covenant:
> blood poured out for sin's forgiveness. R̍.

> As we eat the one bread and share the one cup
> may your Spirit make us one Body
> to proclaim the death of the Lord
> until he comes again in that glory

which reveals the fullness of the kingdom
where through him, in him, and with him,
in the unity of the Spirit and your holy Church,
all glory and honor is yours, almighty Father,
for ever and ever.

All: Amen.

C. Pledging Our Communion in the Sacred Meal

COMMUNION

The *pastor* shows the bread and wine to the concelebrants, saying:

Pastor: Holy things for God's holy people.

All: Happy are we to be invited to this supper.

The *group leaders* prepare for the distribution of the gifts at each table.

The *pastor* breaks one loaf of bread in two, saying:

Pastor: And they recognized him in the breaking of the bread.

The *group leader* gives the bread to group members to the right and to the left, saying:

Group Leader: The Body of Christ.

Communicant: Amen.

The communicant breaks off a piece of the bread, keeps the fragment in hand, and passes the rest of the loaf to the next communicant, saying, "The Body of Christ." When all have been served, they eat together.

The *group leader* passes the cup to the communicant on the right, saying:

Group Leader: The blood of Christ.

Communicant: Amen.

The communicant drinks from the cup and passes it to the next communicant, saying: "The Blood of Christ." The cup is thus shared around the whole table.

While the cups are being passed, the *music minister* leads the total community in a psalm or hymn.

The empty bread baskets and cups are put aside.

PRAYER AFTER COMMUNION

Pastor: Almighty and eternal God,
we have gathered as your people
and proclaimed your Word.
We have found our unity in broken bread
and pledged again our covenant love
in the blood of your Son.
May the celebration of the mysteries of your presence
strengthen us to be the Body of your Son,
Jesus the Christ.

All: Amen.

The *pastor* invites the members of the groups to pray aloud at each table. The *group leaders* direct these prayers for strength to carry the message of this assembly to the world.

Following these prayers, there is a time for silent prayer.

Pastor: Almighty God,
hear these prayers which are uttered
in the name and Spirit of your Son, Jesus Christ,
who lives and rules for ever and ever.

All: Amen.

PART IV: SENDING FORTH

ANNOUNCEMENTS

The *secretary* announces any necessary reminders. At each table, the time of the next meetings of the basic communities is reviewed and any necessary directions repeated.

BLESSING

Presider: Father, Son, and Holy Spirit:
bless us;
keep us in your care;
turn your face to us and have mercy upon us.
Father, Son, and Holy Spirit:
blessed be your name forever!

All: Blessed be God for ever!

DISMISSAL

Leader: Go in peace,
strengthened by word and bread
for the service of all.
Be what you have seen;
proclaim who you are
that they may say of us
even as they said of our ancestors:
"See how they love one another."
God be with you.

CLOSING HYMN

ALTERNATIVE FUTURES FOR THE EUCHARIST

PART II: LITURGY OF THE WORD
SHARED HOMILY: CONVERSATION THAT PUTS COMMUNITIES AT RISK

Bernard J. Lee, S.M.

Introduction

The Word of God is not primarily a voice speaking from an ancient text about a past time. True the sacred text is a voice uttered once upon a time, but it is also a voice that has been turned loose from its original speaker and its original time. When the Word is heard again—really heard—it levies a claim upon immediate lived experience. Whatever levies a new claim now on behalf of a better tomorrow puts today at risk. Did it not do that, it would not yet be God's Word but only a voice from the past. The question is how to be with the words of the Scriptures to give them the best chance to become Word in conversation with us.

The shared homily is certainly one very useful way to help our sacred texts becomes God's real Word. I want to avoid the expression "dialogue homily" because that experience has not always been a happy or useful one. Even when shared homily is simply a freewheeling immediate response to the proclaimed text, we have made a right beginning; we have made the first step towards interpretation. However, we must give the text a chance to interpret us who interpret it. We must let ancient words speak as best they can out of their own world into our world and put us under obligation because of their own character. That takes a special kind of listening and a disciplined mode of conversation. These reflections are about that disciplined mode of conversation.

In the context of this volume, I am thinking of the Liturgy of the Word in its intimate connection with the Liturgy of the Eucharist. But the Word can be celebrated in the way I am suggesting as a self-contained event. It may be used for other texts than the Scriptures. The intimate connection between Word and Eucharist is that they are both offered for consumption, to become the very stuff out of which we are made. Yahweh gave Ezekiel a written scroll to eat: "Son of Man, eat what is given to you, then go speak to the House of Israel." Ezekiel reports, "I opened my mouth; he gave me the scroll to eat and said, 'Son of Man, feed and be satisfied with the scroll I am giving you.' I ate it, and it tasted sweet as honey" (Ezek 3:1-3). We eat the Word and become it; we eat the bread of the Body and become it. Together they are a full course meal!

A good relationship between persons suggests the character of a good relationship between a people and God's Word. That analogy I would like to explore.

There are a lot of ways in which people can be together; some are destructive, and some are creative. I do not mean just occasional encounters but patterns that characterize how people are together creatively or destructively. When people learn which patterns are helpful, they stand a better chance of maintaining quality relationships. A trained ear can often listen in on conversations in a family or among friends and identify the patterns that characterize the whole range of relational interactions. That is precisely because the conversations are the relationship. Just as there are patterns in the way two friends relate, there are patterns in how communities of persons relate. Similarly there are poor ways and effective ways in which a community can attempt conversation with its sacred texts. Hermeneutical theory suggests some patterned ways in which a Christian community can have the kind of relationship with its sacred texts that will help the story it lives be a story of redeemed human experience.

In our time the work of Paul Ricoeur and Hans-Georg Gadamer has had a large influence upon biblical exegesis and theological reflection generally. Their work addresses interpretation: how meaning is wrested from encounters, whether with a text, a tradition, a person, or an event. Interpreting a text has a structure to it that suggests how a community can approach the Word creatively and fruitfully. In the reflections that follow, I will be making applications of both Gadamer's and Ricoeur's work to shared reflection upon Scriptures in the life of an intentional Christian community. For purposes of these reflections, by intentional Christian community I mean small groups of Christians (perhaps five to fifteen in number) who have chosen to be together in regular ways, both for mutual support and for making a difference in how the world goes. The basic Christian community movement in Latin America and the small Christian community movement in East Africa are examples of such intentional Christian communities. The movement is growing within the United States as well, and some indigenous models are emerging. I want to imagine how shared reflection upon the Word might go in such communities, with conversation, as Gadamer understands it, as a key insight.

I shall begin with an analogy: how do people meet, become friends, make meaning together, and maintain a relationship? What can that reveal about a community's encounter with God's Word?

Making Friends

When I meet a new person, I bring with me to that first encounter my own history, expectations, needs, hopes, and aspirations. In other words I already exist in a world of meaning that has been long in the making. I take that world of meaning for granted, rarely reflecting upon it, and presuming that how I understand anything is simply "how things are." The world of meaning that I bring to any new encounter is a preunderstanding that immediately affects the meeting. Although I am seldom aware of it, my preunderstandings greatly shape my initial impressions of a new person. There is no such thing as an uninterpreted experience of anyone or anything. I am interpreting from the first glance and the first sound of a voice. This interpreting is my initial impression of the new person.

If the new person impresses me as interesting, or if circumstances are such that I will over and over meet this person in my life, I may decide to explore the relationship further. If so it soon becomes clear to me that the other person's horizon is not identical to mine, because he has a different history; she has lived a different story. This is normally a painful realization: we do not see everything in the same way; therefore I experience distance. If I am not sufficiently aware that all horizons are conditioned vantage points, I may immediately conclude that "I am right" and "he is wrong," and that is probably the end of that relationship. However, if the other person truly matters, I must do the very hard work of hearing her on her own grounds. I must try to see the world upon a different horizon from my own. Once the difference becomes clear to me, I experience remoteness and distance. There is something in the other's world that is different from mine. It is always very hard work to hear and enter into the otherness of an other. The other is saying to me: "To understand me you must hear me on my own ground." An other who has provoked my attention and interest always levies that kind of claim. I must spend careful time listening to the other's life, and not just the bare events, not just the utterances, but even the structure of the utterances. Structure carries meaning too. So do gestures, facial expressions, tone of voice, rhetoric, and even the pauses and the placement of silences. If I do this long enough and carefully enough, the remoteness named above is gradually broached, though never completely conquered.

I cannot listen seriously to a different life, especially the life of someone who is attractive to me, and come away unchanged. No party to a true conversation comes away unchanged. That is why any authentic conversation is genuinely threatening; I risk being required to alter my sense of things, my understandings, my values, my *self*. The conversation that goes on between friends is a continuing process in which both friends submit their lives to the risks of transformation they know will surely occur. The task of interpretation, whether of an event or a text, is like the task of conversation between friends. It is risky. Processes of careful interpretation put me at risk always and necessarily. I am not only reconstructing and reunderstanding the meaning of my friend (or my sacred text), I am reconstructing the meaning of myself.

Conversation reconstructs the selves that are conversing. That is an incredible risk, and one of the reasons why a "Yes" to the mutuality of relationships is threatening to the core. My meaning is put at risk. Gadamer has rightly understood the depth of risk involved.

Differences and otherness are not doomed to remaining at an irreducible distance. When a friendship is taking shape and growing, there will always be some fusion of our respective horizons. The fusion of horizons is, of course, partly due to the fact that we had from the beginning some shared perceptions and understandings. We surely had some similar history, perhaps because we are both products of Western culture, or because we have the same religious heritage, or because we have some similarities in our nurturing family systems. But there is a more important reason for the fusion of horizons. The reason is that in a true relationship two people become creators of each other's identity. Part of who I am is "your friend," and I only got there by listening to your life on its own grounds, being put at risk, having to change. If our horizons have begun to have some points of fusion (a precondition for deep mutual understanding), it is because we have as friends become cocreators of each other.

Here again the nature of the risk appears. Relationship means cocreation of each other's identity. When there is cocreation, no one person has control. We never really have complete control anyway, but the mutuality of relationships makes the uncontrol clear and asks for an embracing "Yes" to it.

Thus a new relationship always opens up new possibilities for both lives. The conversation of a relationship makes new things appear out in front of the participants. Something is made by the conversation: a possible world is conjured up and projected; a story gets a new plot possibility; history is enriched by a new version of how it might be lived. I may not always think in those terms, but it is nonetheless true.

Possibilities for my life are created by my relationships. A friendship's meaning, therefore, is out in front of us both. In small or large ways every relationship creates possibility. In order to know what a friendship really means for my life, I must understand the possibilities for my life that are projected by the relationship. Exploring the new possibilities opened is not just a flight of fancy. It is an essential act in knowing what someone means for me. Relationships have consequences, and those consequences are its essential meaning. I do not mean that we first understand something and then explore its consequences. I mean that all encounters affect the project called life and that the intuiting of the effects belongs to the act of understanding.

Even though there is some fusion of horizons with my friend, our lives never totally fuse. We remain separate. We continue to grow in our own ways, accumulating new history, some of which will always be outside the particular context of the friendship. We all have other worlds besides the world of a specific relationship. It is inevitable, therefore, that lives that continue to listen to each other will continue to be surprised by each other, for both lives are always in the making.

Someday I come to the relationship with a profound new intuition from today's history, history my friend has not shared, and I have the painful experience of "not feeling understood." I have new initial understandings that condition how I interpret everything. My friend must work hard all over again to enter my new world in order to understand who I am this very day. The process of interpreting begins all over again. Our interpretation shapes our experience and our experience shapes our interpretation. This movement is cyclic in character. It repeats over and over. There is no asking which came first. Interpreting and experiencing are mutually inserted into each other, and together they *are* the relationship. Interpreting is not what we do to understand someone and then we are done with it. Interpreting is experiencing, just as experiencing is interpreting, and these very processes constitute the relationship. The interpreting is the relationship—not less than or other than but simply, the relationship. In this understanding the interpreting is ceaseless. Hans-Georg Gadamer calls this process conversation, the kind of conversation that puts people who engage in it at risk.

This conversation is not a preface to a good relationship; interpreting is the whole story. Tomorrow's possibilities are created by today's conversations. Understanding is never something done once and for all. Understanding is not a noun, it is a verb.

Making Friends with Sacred Texts

The structure of Christian life may be accurately described as the process of making friends with the Christ event. Christian life is a conversation between people and the Christ event, which is constitutive of both Christian life and the Christ event. The process of making friends is not what happens before friendship occurs; the process of making friends goes on and on and on. It is the friendship; the process itself is the reality.

If we are talking about making friends with the Christ event, a word needs to be said about the expression Christ event that has become current in our day. We know today that the various documents of the New Testament are not histories of Jesus so much as histories of multiple early Christian communities remembering Jesus. Raymond Brown has recently asked what happened in the new Christian Churches when the last person who actually knew Jesus had died (*The Church the Apostles Left Behind*, New York: Paulist, 1984). He demonstrates how the New Testament materials reflect many very different solutions to the survival question: how to get along without Jesus and without those who actually knew him. The life, work, teaching, death, and resurrection of Jesus set up a field of force in which many lives joyfully found themselves caught up— so joyfully that they called it good news.

All of our primary canonical documents, therefore, are interpretations of (that is, friendship with) the meaning of Jesus. Because we are not in these documents just encountering Jesus but also the incredible effects of his life upon the world, we must speak in terms of an event that is larger than a single human life that began with birth and ended with death. There are meanings of Jesus that are as old as Abraham and as new as now. The Christ event is temporally thick! Most New Testament scholars tell us that Christ was not a name given Jesus in his historical life on earth. Christ is an interpretation of his meaning of life. Christ is the way the experienced consequences of Jesus were named. *Christ* names many things, and one of them is *the project* that originates out of the life of Jesus. Christ both names Jesus and the project created for people who have conversation with him. Christ is a name for possibilities that are created through friendship with this event. Thus Christ event was an expression created to catch the larger sense of Jesus: whence he came, who he was, what his effects were then, what they are now, and what possibilities are disclosed. Christ interprets the relationship of Jesus to God, of God to us in and through Jesus, of us to each other.

Thus far I have mostly spoken of conversation/interpretation between persons. Keeping that image in mind, I want to speak of conversation with scriptural texts. It is not easy to make friends with Scripture. Doing so is as work laden, as time laden, and as risk laden as any human relationship could ever be.

Anytime we come to the Scriptures, we come with our own histories and all the ways we are conditioned to think, feel, and value by those histories. Yet our preunderstandings are not utterly idiosyncratic. We can have some initial understandings, because there are surely already some shared meanings between us and the Word of God.

However, the Scriptures have horizons that contrast deeply with our contemporary horizons. Some of the Scriptures reflect the experience of very Jewish people responding fully to Jesus, but still fully as Jews. Some of the Scriptures reflect the experience of Jews who had long lived in the diaspora of a Greek-thinking world and were Christian Jews with Athens for a horizon rather than Jerusalem. Some Scriptures reflect the experience of those who were never Jews at all but came to the Christ event from the Graeco-Roman pagan culture. Once I begin to sense that the texts and the structures of the Scriptures can only be understood by letting their meaning be disclosed in their original contexts—as best as that can be recovered and reentered—I start to feel the remoteness of those texts. They have some strangeness about them. Some of the initial familiarity, which felt so comfortable, must be surrendered. We recognize often, when we have encountered a text in its original context, how much interpretation got loaded onto the text from our current preoccupations. What we hear the second time around, after we listened to a text on its own ground, often suggests something quite different than what was conjured up at first hearing. When a text is allowed to speak out of its own world, as best as we are able to let that happen, it nearly always makes quite a different claim upon our lives than it did when we first heard it upon the horizon of our own preoccupations. As we get familiar with the second meaning, some of the remoteness is conquered, and some fusion of horizons becomes possible. Then it is that a new sort of possible world begins to make an appearance out in front of our lives.

It is at this point in our encounter with the Scriptures that we must start asking: what possibilities for lived experience are created by the claims which the newly proclaimed text makes upon us? What is the meaning of the New Testament out in front of the text? The possibilities created by a text met on its own grounds will usually be quite different from a text encountered only on the basis of our initial understandings.

Too often dialogue homilies do not get past the sharing of initial understandings. Initial understandings are not wrong. In fact they are a necessary first step in a good conversation with the text. But they are only a first step. We know how often we feel almost violated when another person takes his/her initial impression and begins to interpret our words and actions without ever having listened closely to our stories on their own grounds. If in those circumstances, where hard listening has not been done, a person encountering me feels a claim for the future, that person is making a claim on him/herself, not one that reflects a possibility for lived experience created by meeting me on my horizon. If we are not respectful enough, we can do that to God's Word, hear what we brought. To be sure it is not only dialogue homilies that may get bogged down in initial understandings and fail to proceed to the

Word on its own ground. Individual homilists are just as suscep-
tible to this form of ventriloquism, hearing only the "voice" of God
that one has uttered oneself.

The Word of God is not words upon a page. The Word is a
word for life, for the project we sometimes call human history. It
is a word for a community's shared life. It is a word that begins
on its own ground, upon its own horizon; it creates a project forward from that place. It is our word and not God's Word, if it did
not create a project starting initially from its own horizon.

Homily as Risky Conversation

Based on the sense of interpretation that I have presented, I will
offer some suggestions for a community's homily. My own experience suggests that the shared homily restrict itself to a single
text. If two texts are considered, the considerations should be separate unless there is some intimate internal linkage, for example,
a New Testament text that makes explicit reference to an Old Testament text. I will now describe the structure of the three essential
subevents of a dialogue homily which together constitute a friend-
making process with the Christ event: first, identifying and naming our initial understandings of a text; second, trying to let the
text meet us out of its own world and working toward a fusion of
horizons, ours and the text's; and third, probing the claims upon
lived experience that emerge from conversation with the text, the
text's out front meaning.

Initial Understandings

Psychologists can often listen to the patterns in a family's conversation and sense whether they are healthy or destructive. The
patterns are there, even though they are seldom anything of which
anyone is consciously aware. There are also patterns in the conversations we have with God's Word. Hermeneutical theory suggests that a really productive conversation with a text is a disciplined,
nuanced, and rigorous procedure. At first its practitioners find its
details artificial, restraining, and self-conscious, but sufficiently prac-
ticed it becomes second instinct as a "friendship behavior" with a
sacred text. In what follows I want to suggest such a conversational
pattern, based on what has gone before in these reflections.

First, the text is proclaimed, perhaps a second and third time.
Participants may also have their own copies of the text. After this
there is a period for quiet reflection. Then all participants are in-

vited to give their initial responses to what was heard—not measured and weighed responses, just the immediate feelings and thoughts
which the proclaimed text conjures up. This is not meant to be an
analysis of the text or the situation. This sharing is not about the
text but about us who heard the text. The kinds of questions that
are important are such as these: what impression did you have; what
words grabbed your attention; what feelings were experienced; what
mood did the text evoke in you. It is helpful to have facilitators
prompt the discussion, but they must be careful not to inject any
of their interpretation as facilitator. Presiding at the Word in the
ways suggested here is one possible function of a minister of the
Word, a service into which lector can evolve. When community
members know each other well and have some shared history, they
may not need a prompter; they may share in the ministry of the
Word.

The group should be small enough so that all participants can
have their say, and all should. If the group is much larger than fifteen, this reading might be done once for everybody. But then
smaller units are formed for sharing the initial understandings. It
would be possible in a parish setting to have one small group go
through all of these procedures with the congregation observing and
experiencing that small group.

Why a group? Why should we not hear the Word and go through
these procedures on our own? There is a very good, perhaps even
an essential reason for the group. Our preunderstandings look to
us so matter-of-fact that their presuppositional status is almost impossible to detect. It is only when I hear an interpretation different
from my own that I stand a chance of recognizing my presuppositions and therefore of admitting the relativized and partial character of my horizon. I am awed at what another sees that I myself
did not see. I am surprised by an almost opposite interpretation
from my own. On the other hand, I am sometimes reassured by
striking similarities. Encountering contrasting interpretations "loos-
ens us up" and makes it easier to hear the text on its own grounds
in the next step, especially if we have seen how our own desires
and needs colored what we initially found there. There are things
about ourselves and our presuppositions that are impossible to learn
except in the white heat of dialogic moments.

Not only do individuals have preunderstandings. So do communities with accumulated history. Not all the work in the world
can nudge individuals or communities completely free of all presup-

positions. We can never recognize all the layers of historical conditioning. We can only become aware of some of it and be better dispossessed of interpretive imperialism by knowing that many of our presuppositions will always elude us.

The discovery of how our preunderstandings shape our initial understandings may or may not immediately help the texts to speak out of their world (more work needs to be done for that to happen), but there is another immediate benefit for a community. Preunderstandings are such a part of our deep story, that getting them named is a way of getting our stories out into the open for each other to see and to hold. Moments of deep story exposure are moments of great vulnerability. But if that occurs in the context of celebrating the Word, then the chances of vulnerability happening in benevolent, graced time and space is very huge indeed.

There is a second reason for the power of a group in making friends with the Christ event. That reason is that we are relational beings, social in every dimension of our lives. We have no private vocations. We exist first, last, and always as parts of a relational web. Nothing affects any individual that does not reverberate throughout all parts of the web. In Christian metaphor together we are a Body. In sociological terms we are a social system. The Word of God is always an address to social systems fully as much as to individual Christians, because individuals live only and always in social systems. A people receives the Word, and persons receive the Word always as parts of a people, members of a Body radically interconnected with other members of the same Body. It is indeed healthy, holy, and necessary for all individuals to spend time alone with the Word, but if they are accosted by it while alone, they are still accosted in all their social reality. Since the community also, as community, is addressed by God's Word, is it essential that it bring itself in its "social system" dimensions to profound conversation with that Word.

The first part of a shared homily, then, is the laying out of our initial understandings, as individuals and as community, in response to hearing the Scriptures proclaimed. We must become aware of how our preunderstandings affect what we first hear so that we can better come to the text with clean ears to hear what it says from its own vantage point.

THE TEXT ON ITS OWN GROUNDS

For interpretation distance is both a problem and a gift. It is a problem, because it heralds separateness and otherness. It is a gift, because distance is what makes interpretation possible. Once recognized and accepted otherness can be approached and broached for exactly what it is: difference. The distance also makes clear the kind of work that must be done if some of the remoteness is to be overcome.

Many forms of biblical studies have emerged in recent decades to help conquer some of the remoteness of the biblical world: form criticism, editorial criticism, literary criticism, structural analysis, to name some. All of these studies help the contemporary hearer of the Word enter a little more effectively into the world in which the Word was originally spoken. These studies have also created a place for a new kind of leadership in community. The community needs people with that kind of background to guide their sensibilities. With the help of historical biblical studies, it is easier to meet the text on its own ground.

Let me give two short examples. The English words "hate" and "divorce" are not identical, but they do have a meaning in common; they both imply deliberate distancing, choices made about separate ways. When "hate" is used in divorce proceedings in ancient Hebrew materials, the emphasis in the Hebrew word is not upon strong negative affect but upon going separate ways. "I hate you" seems to mean, "By our decisions our lives will part and each will take a separate road through life." There may indeed be feelings of revulsion and vindictiveness. That, however, is not the primary meaning the word is intended to carry, although it may carry those meanings as well. When this word is translated into Greek or Latin or English, there is no word in any of these languages that is freighted with meaning identical to the Hebrew Word. When Jesus says that to be his follower one must "hate" mother and father, hate is a poor translation (and "leave" is not strong enough). It means something more akin to radical separation, lives that may not be lived on the same street, or in the same village, or out of the same values. The word implies radical choice to move on one's own wherever one has to go to follow Christ. Most people's initial response to the Scripture text is one of horror, that following Jesus means hating one's parents. But when the words are heard on their own ground, they call one to radical choice and not to the rejection of one's parents. That is but a small example of the difference it makes to let words speak out of their own world of meaning if they are to make a legitimate claim today.

As a second example let us take the familiar story of the Good Samaritan. It is not uncommon for hospitals to be named Good Samaritan Hospital. That conjures up the notion of care for the sick. Nor is it uncommon for someone who performed a notable good service for someone else to be called a "Good Samaritan" in a newspaper article about the matter. Culturally Good Samaritan has come to carry the meaning of doing a good deed for someone. From that cultural matrix a hearer of Luke's parable may well conclude that we are placed under requirement to heal the sick or do good for our neighbor. In my experience these are the kinds of reflections that tend to come out when people share their initial responses to the story. In the Lukan account there is no mention of the long history of bitterness, distrust, and hatred that characterized the feelings of Jews and Samaritans for one another, even though that is the story's essential horizon. However, the parable cannot levy its true claim unless it is heard against that background. In our age unfortunately and tragically Americans tend to see any Russian or communist as a bitter enemy, an implacable foe. If a wounded American lay on a New York street, seen but passed by unattended by American after American, and if that American were then to be seen by a member from the Soviet delegation to the United Nations who took him to the hospital and paid the bill, the true power of the parable would begin to emerge. The Good Samaritan is one whose splendid mercies reach out to heal the perceived enemy precisely because we are all children of the same God. The parable in fact seems to want to retire the word enemy from a Christian's structure of experience. The Jew/Samaritan analogy with American/Soviet hints at the fusion of horizons that makes new meanings come out of the Good Samaritan story. Without that fusion of horizons, the meaning out in front of the text has to do with caring for the sick with immense generosity. However, when the words speak out of their own cultural matrix, the project suggested by Jesus calls for a stature of spirit that transcends categories of friend and enemy. The project suggested by the first interpretation is neither bad nor incorrect; it is simply not a full enough grasp of Jesus' meaning to hear Jesus on his own ground, nor is it ample enough in its demands to redeem historical experience in the manner called for by Jesus' words.

A shared homily that is a true conversation with the Christ event can profit greatly from the leadership of someone equipped to guide a community's sensibilities into another world, the world of the text.

This does not mean that every community must have a Scripture scholar. But it does imply a new kind of minister of the Word and a new sense of community need for someone so prepared. Perhaps the Jewish model of Torah study is a better image than that of the Western scholar. The study of the Torah for a Jew is not primarily a quest for knowledge but an act of worship. Studying the Scriptures IS worship. The new ministers of the Word in the kind of shared homily under consideration have "gone into the Scriptures" so that when they come into community, they enter it with that world and are able to present it.

There can be no genuine conversation if one has not first made an effort to hear what is said upon its own horizon. That is a precondition for interpretation, but is not yet interpretation.

In both of the examples just given, we already moved from hearing what a text says on its own grounds to what claims it makes on tomorrow when it has been heard thus. The way I have divided up the progressive pieces of a shared homily is indeed somewhat artificial, because all these moments of the process presuppose each other and color each other. Yet there are distinguishable subevents to the larger event of interpretation, and we pass now to a focus upon how texts have meanings out in front of them.

Meaning "Out in Front"

The work indicated in the previous section intended, as it were, to get "behind the text." That, however, is but a start. The important thing is getting ahead of the text, finding its meaning out in front, letting its forward intention become manifest. When that occurs, a text has escaped the intention of the first speaker and the attention of the first hearer. We do all we can to stand on the original horizon. But those words can never again mean exactly the same thing to us as when they first crashed into history and built the edifice of someone's life. We live in a new world. We listen with new ears. Our lives are thrust upon a new horizon. Yet there can still be an encounter with that early world and its horizon. That other horizon and our horizon can begin to fuse in genuine conversation. When that happens, new meaning is made. This meaning is out in front of the Scripture text, not buried behind it or underneath it. It speaks of a new tale to be told.

When the Pharisees explored the Scriptures—the Torah—to find out how to be in the world in new ways, they called their interpretations *Halakhah*, a word etymologically related to road or way. They were marking out a road to be taken. One of the earliest names for the Christian message was the Way. It is a way that leads ahead; it is a projection. Projection of a way is intrinsic to the text's meaning. In fact the words do not truly become Word until some Way appears. God's Word transforms what it finds, sometimes ever so gently, sometimes like a torrent, sometimes like a fire. But whether it accosts gently or vehemently, accost it does. I sometimes fantasize a new set of rubrics for the minister of the Word. I imagine that after the words of Scripture have been proclaimed and reflected upon, the minister asks those who were accosted to raise their hands. The new rubric which I imagine tells the minister of the Word that if no one was accosted, the minister may not say, "This is the Word of God." Instead the minister would say, "This might have been the Word of God. It may yet be the Word of God. So far today it does not seem to have become the Word of God." The accosting must be made by the Word from its horizon, by an interaction with us on our horizon, until some fusion of horizons has been provoked by the conversation, that is, until there is a strong meeting in present time in which the character of all participants in the conversation is honored.

In this third moment of shared homily, after initial understandings have been shared, after the words of Scripture have been located upon their horizons, participants are invited to share their new response to the text: what does the world before me look like because of the Word I have heard or the horizons that have met? How is our going forth ("Go now to love and serve the Lord!") illuminated by the Word that has been received?

The minister of the Word should at this juncture of the interpretive process encourage a certain pragmatism. It is life as actually lived that is accosted. It is a world in all its particularity that is addressed. The Word of God is not generic! It is occasion specific! It is not as specific as some one and only decision that must be made. The Word often illumines a range of real possibility, not just one single best possibility. But it deals with this life, this world, this history. It is not alongside of history. It is a Word that speaks out of lived experience in the idiom of historical existence. Its accents sound like people's lives sound. The projection that is intrinsic to the Word's meaning must be kept in touch with the ways that actual situations might truly be moved. It is not mere fanciful speculation. And I stress the word mere, because there are ways indeed in which fantasy keeps thinking lives open to God when God does something unthinkable. The minister of the Word, in the structure being recommended here, should encourage projection not just about things generally but about "these things" in "this world" by "these people."

A true homily and a true prayer have in common with conversation that they put the participants at risk. We never know what will happen. There is an Hasidic story about a rabbi who would put his last will and testament in order before every sabbath, because he did not know whether he would emerge from prayer alive. When we say yes to a relationship, we do not know what parts of us will live and which will die, nor how the living parts will be changed. Because Jewish faith insists upon God and people as cocreators of history, with God's Spirit and Word as principal agents from God's side, God's project is also put at risk; he does not know the outcome of his conversation with our lives. Prayer and the Liturgy of the Word are each a dialectic meeting of two powers, two collaborators. The two powers are asymmetrical in their respective efficacy, but nonetheless they are two separate powers that meet in conversation.

Let us return now to our shared homily. In our community conversation we first shared and heard each other's initial understandings. Then we backed away some from our presuppositions, as best we could, and heard the text on its own ground. We felt its remoteness, which having been partially conquered became its nearness. It spoke in our ears again; it made the world today look different; it accosted tomorrow's world. In some small or large way a new tale to be told was created in conversation with the sacred story. Our community once again interpreted its sacred texts. The words of the sacred text have now become the Word of the living God.

Conclusion

Hermeneutical theory has helped us understand both how better to interpret our sacred texts and also what hard work it is. The shared homily proposed here for use in intentional communities is not just an animated discussion but a disciplined process aimed at giving God's Word power to build our lives and our world. In the early stages of a community's life, this procedure feels labored and artificial; the three steps are all necessary. With enough use, however, it becomes an instinct and not a program. To summarize:

1. The text is slowly proclaimed. Those assembled then name their most immediate responses to the text. The presiding minister of the Word tries to help the community identify the worlds of meaning which they brought with them and which gave some shaping to how they initially understood the text.

2. The minister of the Word tries to offer the kind of "background briefing" that helps the words of the text speak from the worlds in which they were first uttered. This must not be a classroom lecture on historical biblical criticism, yet it must deal as amply as possible with whatever introduces the words' own horizon. An easy narrative style is most helpful—lecturing violates liturgical mood!

3. Then the text is proclaimed once again. The community attempts to feel what these words, situated upon their own horizon, have to do with today. Together they probe the meaning out in front of the text. They are interested in knowing where the horizon of the words first spoken begins to intersect with the horizon of the lives who have just heard the words again. They ask what is the tale to be told by their lives, individually and communally, now that they have been accosted by the words of a sacred text.

If the Liturgy of the Word is followed by the Liturgy of the Eucharist, the tale to be told may effectively be reevoked at the time of dismissal, for that moment is in fact a time of missioning: "Go forth from here now, but carry the Good News with you from here into your actual world." The mission means more when it has a concrete configuration, when it addresses immediate lived experience, when it means something out there in front of the lives we are living.

It is important in actual use that each of the steps be consciously taken. If we do not first get in touch with our presuppositions, our needs, our prejudices, and our present worlds, we will have a very difficult time hearing through them to the Word with its own presuppositions, needs, and prejudices. If we mistake our own for those of the Word, then the voices we hear are likely to be our own. But we will call them the Word of God, because as unconscious ventriloquists we will not even have recognized our own voices.

These suggestions for shared homily may be used as Liturgy of the Word in conjunction with Liturgy of the Eucharist, or as Liturgy of the Word in its own right, or as part of a discernment process in a meeting of any intentional Christian community. In any event the words are not Word until we, in our personal and communal existence, are placed by them upon the Way, until we are signaled towards a road to be taken, until the energies of our being are committed to a tale to be told.

References

Bernstein, Richard J. *Beyond Objectivism and Relativism: Science, Hermeneutics, and Praxis.* Philadelphia: University of Pennsylvania Press, 1983.

Gadamer, Hans-Georg. *Truth and Method.* New York: Crossroads, 1975.

Grant, Robert, and Tracy, David. *A Short History of the Interpretation of the Bible,* especially Tracy's chapters 16, 17 and 18. Philadelphia: Fortress Press, 1984.

Palmer, Richard E. *Hermeneutics.* Evanston Ill.: Northwestern University Press, 1965.

Ricoeur, Paul. *Hermeneutics and the Human Sciences.* London: Cambridge University Press, 1981.

Ricoeur, Paul. *Interpretation Theory.* Fort Worth: Texas Christian University Press, 1976.

Ricoeur, Paul. *The Rule of Metaphor.* Toronto: University of Toronto Press, 1984.

Rorty, Richard. *Philosophy and the Mirror of Nature.* Princeton: Princeton University Press, 1979.

Thistleton, Anthony C. *The Two Horizons.* Grand Rapids: Eerdmans, 1980.

Index

Acts of the Apostles, 60–61
American culture, 51–52, 76
American economy, 49, 76
Austin, Gerard, 120

Baptism, 18, 55, 59–60, 67, 90, 98, 103
Basic communities. *See* Intentional communities
Bishops of the United States and unions, 109
Body of Christ as community, 17, 58–60, 62–63, 65, 66, 68, 70, 72, 74–75, 80, 120, 126, 145, 167
Bultmann, Rudolf, 95

Catholic immigration to America, 108
Charisms, 64–65
Christ, allegiance to, 77–79
Code of Canon Law, 124
Communitarian consciousness, 50, 57, 63, 66–68
Communitarian theology of the sacraments, 99
Community, types of, 25–26
Conference of Saint Serge, Paris, (1976), 120
Conscience, 37, 70
Constitution on the Sacred Liturgy, 41, 118–19, 126, 134
Corinthian Eucharist, 52–57
Corinthians, First Letter of Paul to, 52–56, 58–59, 61–72, 78–81, 94
Corinthians, Second Letter to the, 61–62
Crocker, Jon Christopher, 37
Cultural pluralism, 19, 40–42

Decree on Ecumenism, 101–2
Demons, 71–72
Diakonia, 62–63
Divino Afflante Spiritu, 87

Eastern Churches, 102
"Economic Justice for All," pastoral letter of the American bishops, 50
Economism, 50, 77
Ecumenical movement, 102, 104, 108
Ernesti, Johann August, 32
Eschatological movements, 29
Existentialism, 87–88, 95–96, 98, 104

Gadamer, Hans-Georg, 158–60, 162
Galatians, Letter to the, 56, 72–73
Gemeinschaft, 26, 75
Gesellschaft, 26, 75
Gifford Lectures, 34
Good Samaritan, lessons of the story of, 169

Hardy, Sir Alister, 34
Heidegger, Martin, 87, 95
Historical consciousness pertaining to sacraments, 86
Holy Spirit, 59, 61, 67

Individualism, 20–21
Intentional communities (basic communities), 12–14, 17–18, 21, 25–29, 31, 38, 40, 45–46, 49–50, 75–76, 79, 101, 105, 107, 117, 120–21, 128, 145, 159, 172–73

James, William, 10, 34
John, First Letter of, 60, 72
John Paul II, Pope, 50, 58

Kavanagh, Aidan, 13
Kennedy, John F., 106
Koinonia, 57, 60–63, 65–66, 71–72, 80–81
Kuhn, Thomas, 104

Last Supper as a Passover meal, 92–93
Leo XIII, Pope, 87
Liberation theology, 88, 99, 104, 108
Lima document on baptism, the Eucharist, and ministry, 102–3
Love, 63–65, 70, 80–81

"Mass for Theatre," by Leonard Bernstein, 10
Mead, Margaret, 43
Merleau-Ponty, Maurice, 97
Messianic movements, 29
Michel, Virgil, 15, 111

Nicene Creed, 103

Orate Fratres (Worship), 108

Paul, St., 52–73, 77–78, 80–81, 105
Pauline eschatology, 81
Phenomenology, 87–88, 95–97, 104
Philippians, Letter to the, 61, 78
Privatism, 19–20
Process modes of thought, 88, 98
Prophets of the Old Testament, 35–36

Rahner, Karl, 90, 95–96
Real presence in the Eucharist, 95
Relationship of Catholics and Protestants, 109
"Religion of escape," 38–39

Religious freedom, 109
Revelation, 24
Ricoeur, Paul, 158–59
Rite of Christian Initiation of Adults (RCIA), 13
"Ritual-as-action," 37
"Ritual-as-belief," 37
Romans, Letter to the, 59, 64, 71, 81

Sacraments, social dimension of, 88
Sacrifices to idols, 68–69, 71, 79
St. John's Abbey, Collegeville, Minnesota, 15, 85–86, 108
Scripture study as worship, 170
Second Vatican Council, 51, 73, 77, 86, 89, 91, 95, 100–3, 108–9, 110, 118
Secularism, 21–22, 32
Shared homily, 157, 164–65, 167, 169, 171–73
Split consciousness, 77
Symbols, 36

Tonnies, Ferdinand, 26
Transignification, 96–97
Transubstantiation, 74, 97, 103, 120, 127
Transubstantiation of the assembly, 120, 127
Trinity, beginning of concept in New Testament, 61

United States Constitution, 20

Value systems, 39–40

Whitehead, Alfred North, 88
Women in the Church, 110
Worship of idols, 71